ARE YOU CAPABLE
OF COMPROMISE?

No one doubts that a successful, loving relationship requires some sacrifices. But you don't have to be a saint or a martyr to make love work. Answer the following questions to learn whether you can balance your needs with those of someone else:

* Your partner is involved in a special project at work and will be home a few hours later than usual. What do you do?

* What's your philosophy and practice concerning giving to charity?

* Do you usually get gifts you like?

* If you were given a grade for taking care of yourself, what would it be?

* You're having lunch with a friend at one of your favorite restaurants. She's on a strict diet. You're craving their famous chocolate raspberry mousse. Do you order it?

* When you were growing up, how important was it for you to please your parents?

To score your answers, and to find out how successful you are at compromise, see Chapter 7. Your revealing profile—and strategies to improve it—are here in the book that's basic training for love!

Books by Ellen Lederman

Perfect Partners: The Couples Compatibility Guide
Are You Ready for Love?

Published by POCKET BOOKS

ARE YOU READY FOR LOVE?

Discover the Skills of Romance

ELLEN LEDERMAN

POCKET BOOKS

New York London Toronto Sydney Tokyo Singapore

An *Original* publication of Pocket Books

 POCKET BOOKS, a division of Simon & Schuster Inc.
1230 Avenue of the Americas, New York, NY 10020

Lederman, Ellen, 1954–
    Are you ready for love? : discover the skills of romance / Ellen
Lederman.
        p.   cm.
    Includes bibliographical references.
    ISBN: 0-671-73464-4 : $9.00
    1. Love.   2. Interpersonal relations.   I. Title.
HQ801.L368   1992
158'.2—dc20   91-39107
                                                         CIP

First Pocket Books trade paperback printing June 1992

10 9 8 7 6 5 4 3 2 1

Love doesn't make the world go around.
Love is what makes the ride worthwhile.
FRANKLIN P. JONES

CONTENTS

Before you started first grade, you had to meet certain prerequisites. Your parents had to present official papers, such as a birth certificate, as well as proof of required immunizations. By the end of kindergarten, you had to master important preacademic skills ranging from knowing colors and shapes to getting along with peers. If you had not attained these skills, entrance into the first grade may have been delayed. Another year of kindergarten may have been recommended to ready you for the demands of school.

As you matured, you were faced with other tests and measurements of preparedness. You had to pass your driving test to prove that you were ready to assume the responsibility of being behind the wheel. If you were college bound, there was no avoiding the SAT or ACT as one of the primary determinants of whether you would be accepted by the college of your choice. Once you completed your education, further standardized tests may have awaited you to assess your readiness to practice certain professions.

But love is the one area of your life in which your prerequisite skills were never evaluated. Aside from your parents dictating in your teenage years when you would be allowed to start dating, no one attempted to judge whether or not you were ready for love. You probably didn't give much thought to it, either. You only knew that you, like almost everyone else in the world, wanted love in your life. If it came your way, you probably didn't hesitate to jump into a relationship. And when love wasn't a part of your life, chances are you spent a great deal of time and energy looking for it.

Wanting love does not necessarily mean that you're ready for love, however. The high incidence of unsuccessful marriages and relationships suggest that many people lack some of the skills and traits needed for loving and for being loved. The problem is that most of us simply don't know how to determine our readiness for love. Because it's such an emotionally charged issue, it's difficult to evaluate ourselves objectively in terms of our romantic strengths and weaknesses. Yet without this knowledge, it's next to impossible to improve any deficiencies so that love can become more available and more satisfying.

Happily, it's now possible to assess your personal aptitude for love. This book is designed to help you do just that. *Are You Ready for Love?* offers you the opportunity to learn where you stand in terms of ten crucial components of the abilities to love and be loved. Quizzes at the beginning of each chapter will show whether you have too much, too little, or just the right amount of the skills or personality trait in question. In-depth profiles explain how your characteristics apply in life and love. Should you learn that you need to improve in a particular area, the strategies section at the end of each chapter provides unique and specific suggestions for developing your love ability.

Whether you're currently looking for love or are already involved in a relationship, you'll want to read every chapter to gain a complete understanding of your readiness for love. It's easy, fun, and enlightening . . . and it just might help you find love, or make it even better!

ARE
YOU
READY
FOR
LOVE?

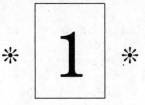

Are You Willing to Take a Chance on Love?

Life always involves some degree of risk. Traffic accidents, natural disasters, criminal acts and illness can happen to any of us, even if we live as carefully as possible. There's no way to avoid risk entirely. Engineers and scientists can introduce safety measures into the way we eat, exercise, and travel, but there will never be an absolute guarantee that we'll always be safe and happy.

While risk is inherent in every part of life, it's especially prevalent in the area of love. Becoming involved and remaining in a relationship is a gamble. Even professional matchmakers can't assure their clients of living happily ever after. The high divorce rate among the general population reflects the risk associated with love and marriage. Obviously, many of the couples whose relationships end in divorce were either not ready for love or chose the wrong partners. They took a chance on love and lost.

What are the risks of loving and being loved? There are some that may be specific to your relationship, but most are universal. These include:

- Getting hurt.
- Being rejected.

- Suffering an emotional or financial loss if the relationship ends.
- Putting more into the relationship than you get out of it.
- Choosing the wrong person.
- Catching a sexually transmitted disease.
- Losing your independence and freedom.
- Becoming disappointed and disillusioned if love doesn't live up to your expectations.

Since all the above risks are possible any time you enter into or stay in a relationship, it's only natural you would feel some apprehension about love. What's important, though, is how you deal with your fears. If you recognize them, but don't allow them to interfere with a loving relationship, there shouldn't be any problem. Should you ignore them and deny their existence, you may be in danger of proceeding recklessly into a relationship that may be wrong for you. You might also fail to exercise due caution once in a relationship. And if you're so threatened by even the remotest possibility of risk that it immobilizes you from ever taking a chance, you may be reluctant to immerse yourself in love fully.

The amount of risk you're comfortable with in your everyday living reflects your risk-taking attitudes toward love. Take the following quiz and learn where you stand in terms of risk-taking or risk-avoiding.

✳   **Q U I Z**   ✳

Choose the answer that best describes the action you would take in each situation.

1. While driving on the highway ten to fifteen miles above the speed limit, you notice that several cars are pulled over to the side of the road and are being ticketed by the police. What would you do?
   a. Slow down for a few miles and then speed up again.
   b. Drive under the speed limit for the rest of the trip.
   c. Continue driving at the same speed.

2. You've invited the new man in your life to dinner and want to prepare a special meal. The dessert you plan to make is:
   a. One you've never had before. You choose something that sounds wonderfully decadent from a gourmet magazine or cookbook.
   b. A favorite recipe from a friend or relative. It's something you've always enjoyed but have never gotten around to making yourself.
   c. Something tried-and-true. You've been making this cake for years and have always been complimented on it.

3. You've come to realize that you're tired of your job. The challenges and excitement have long been over. You check with the personnel department and learn that you could liquidate your pension plan if you resigned and have an amount equal to six months of your salary. You would:
   a. Change jobs, staying in the same field in the same town. (And you wouldn't leave your current job until you had a new one.)
   b. Quit your job, move to a city you've always wanted to live in, and look for a new job.
   c. Stay where you are. After all, you like the people and the money isn't bad.

4. It's time to start planning for your vacation. This summer you'll:
   a. Vacation the same way you usually do (e.g., same or similar beach house, condo in the mountains, cruise to the Caribbean, etc.).
   b. Go somewhere you've never been, but with friends who are familiar with the area.
   c. Try some new and exotic adventure that you've heard or read about.

5. A new restaurant has just opened in your neighborhood. It looks like it could be interesting. You'd be most likely to:
   a. Try it immediately.
   b. Wait until a friend or restaurant critic recommends it.
   c. Wait a few weeks to see if it becomes popular and then patronize it if lots of other people are doing the same.

6. You inherit ten thousand dollars and want to invest it. You would choose:
   a. Blue-chip stocks, municipal bonds, and mutual funds.

    b. Bank CDs or treasury notes.
    c. Commodities, futures, high-tech stocks, or junk bonds.

7. There's a new color that's becoming popular this year. It's one you've never used in your house but you find it very appealing. You would:
    a. Paint the walls or reupholster the couch in the same color.
    b. Continue to admire it in the stores but leave well enough alone and not make any changes in your decorating scheme.
    c. Buy some throw pillows or a vase in the new color.

8. You've read all the warnings about the dangers of too much sun and how it can cause wrinkles and skin cancer. How do you respond to this information?
    a. Avoid being outside as much as possible.
    b. Modify your sunning by avoiding the strongest rays between eleven A.M. and two A.M. and use a sunblock lotion.
    c. Ignore it and continue to be a sun worshipper. (There's always Retin-A if you start to wrinkle.)

9. Would you be willing to go out on a blind date?
    a. Never! You'd rather curl up in front of the TV with your cat.
    b. Why not? It's just one evening out of your life and you never have to see him or her again if you don't want to.
    c. Only if he or she was highly recommended by one of your closest friends.

10. If you were attending an international festival, what would you have for lunch?
    a. Food you've had a few times before (which you know you like), such as Greek gyros or Japanese tempura.
    b. Something you've never tried before (e.g., Ethiopian doro wot, Korean barbecue or fried yucca from El Salvador).
    c. The usual burger, fries, ice cream, etc.

11. You made plans months ago for a trip to Central America. Now you've been reading in the newspaper that one of the countries you had planned to visit is experiencing some social and political unrest. What's your next step?
    a. Change your plans, omitting the country that may be having some trouble and increasing your time in the other countries.
    b. Cancel the whole trip and make arrangements to visit Disney World.

    c. Follow your original itinerary (unless the federal government forbids its citizens from traveling to the particular country in turmoil).

12. You spot an attractive man in the grocery store. He looks familiar. You think you may have gone to school with him but you aren't a hundred percent sure. You would:

    a. Go up to him and ask if he went to your school.

    b. Walk by him and try to catch his eye, waiting to see if *he* recognizes *you* and says something.

    c. Convince yourself that you must be mistaken and finish your shopping.

SCORING

Total up your points to the twelve questions as follows:

1. a- 3	b- 1	c- 5
2. a- 5	b- 3	c- 1
3. a- 3	b- 5	c- 1
4. a- 1	b- 3	c- 5
5. a- 5	b- 1	c- 3
6. a- 3	b- 1	c- 5
7. a- 5	b- 1	c- 3
8. a- 1	b- 3	c- 5
9. a- 1	b- 5	c- 3
10. a- 3	b- 5	c- 1
11. a- 3	b- 1	c- 5
12. a- 5	b- 3	c- 1

41 to 60—Risk-taker
29 to 40—Risk-evaluator
12 to 28—Risk-avoider

✳ Profiles

Find the profile that corresponds to your quiz score.

RISK-TAKER

There's no doubt you're a fearless risk-taker. The prospect of something new or even slightly dangerous doesn't bother you in the least; in fact, the challenge invigorates you. Taking chances in your life makes you feel alive. You'd be bored and restless if everything were always predictable and safe.

The advantages of being a risk-taker are many. Your willingness to explore the unknown enables you to discover exciting new people and places before the rest of the crowd knows about them. Other people wait until a vacation spot or restaurant becomes trendy, but by that time both the price and crowds increase significantly. You get to enjoy them while they're just beginning to get established.

Best of all for you as a risk-taker are the emotional highs you experience. Because you're determined not to let life ever become boring, you constantly seek out ways to put more zest into living. You thrive on the exhilaration that comes from going out on a limb and succeeding against the odds. Your successes reinforce your self-esteem and enable continued personal growth. Since you feel good about yourself and your life, you refuel your courage to continue risking.

The payoffs of risk-taking in love can be tremendous. Your openness to new people and experiences leads to an abundance of acquaintances, thus providing you with a large pool of potential partners. Consider yourself fortunate that you're not limited to a small number of candidates. The chances of your finding the right person to love and be loved by are that much greater when you choose from many instead of only a few.

Your willingness to put yourself on the line and make yourself vulnerable leads to an intensity in your relationships that risk-avoiders may never know. You're likely to have a rich love life because you don't hold back. Both in and out of bed, you fearlessly plunge ahead into new, unexplored sexual and emotional territory. Communication and passion are seldom missing in a risk-taker's relationships.

But there *is* a downside to risking. Success is far from guaranteed in any aspect of life. Whenever you put yourself on the line and take a chance, there's the possibility that things won't go as you had hoped. You could fail, and the failure could be substantial. Your investment decisions could backfire and result in a serious loss of your money. If you bet your life savings at Las Vegas, mountain climb in a snowstorm, or lay out in the sun all day despite all the warnings, you're flirting with possible disastrous consequences. The more you risk, the more you can lose: your self-confidence, money, job security, relationships, or even life or limb.

Love is always very chancy. A relationship needs careful nurturing to continue and succeed. As a risk-taker, you may never have developed any sense of caution. Action, rather than thought, is more your style, so you're apt to behave recklessly at times. When choosing a love partner, you may not use good judgment and may instead choose someone impulsively, or for all the wrong reasons. Even if you do find the right partner, you might say or do something that could hurt him or her and cause an irreparable rift between the two of you. Either scenario could eventually become painful for both you and your partner.

To prevent your risk-taking from interfering with your ability to love and be loved, learn to control your risk-taking impulses to enhance, rather than hurt, your relationship. Read the strategies section on "Controlling Your Risk-Taking" for suggestions on effective risking.

RISK-EVALUATOR

Neither an extreme risk-taker nor a risk-avoider, you've developed a healthy balance between the two. You do take risks sometimes, and you avoid risks at others. The determining factor in your risking is your analysis of the risk-reward ratio. Instead of automatically taking a chance or refusing to take a chance based on a set pattern of dealing with risk, you evaluate every situation on an individual basis. When you believe that the potential rewards outweigh any possible negative consequences, you willingly risk. When your chances for success seem slim compared to the potential for failure or significant emotional or physical harm, you usually choose not to risk.

Your ability to analyze risks isn't something you've developed overnight. There's no magical mathematical formula that enables you to know when taking a chance is okay and when it's not. All you do is base your analysis on what you've learned from your own—as well as other people's—past experiences. Considering each risk and its potential for reward isn't even something you do on a conscious level. More often than not, a gut-level instinct tells you to proceed or warns you to pull back.

There will be times when you'll make the wrong decision. You'll decide to risk and something will go wrong. In hindsight, you'll realize that maybe you shouldn't have taken the risk. Or you'll choose not to take a chance and later regret missed opportunities. But on the whole, you should be fairly satisfied with how you live your life.

Risking when you shouldn't have and not risking when you should have balance each other out and help you to avoid major trauma. Your life will have a good dose of stability, and you'll allow enough room for growth as well. There will be predictability, but also variety and novelty.

The moderation that you apply to risk-taking is usually apparent in your approach to love. You may be mildly cautious about who you get involved with, but once you develop a relationship, you're not adverse to taking a few risks to help the relationship grow. You don't mind being the first to say "I love you," and you don't shy away from becoming vulnerable. You'll lay your deepest feelings on the line as you reveal them to your partner. While you're well aware there are no guarantees in love, you're convinced it's well worth the risk.

You'll take the necessary risks to keep love fresh and rewarding while making sure not to take any undue risks that could compromise your relationship. Fortunately, you're skilled at recognizing behaviors and attitudes that can diminish or destroy love. Whereas risk-takers might find themselves doing things that hurt their relationships (often without meaning to), you're careful to make sure that this doesn't happen to you. Risk-evaluators aren't likely to take any foolish chances with their relationships. Betraying a partner's trust by being unfaithful is not a risk-evaluator's style. Neither is saying hurtful things that can't be unsaid after the argument is over. Knowing love is fragile, you go out of your way to avoid negative actions or words that could interfere with your ability to love and be loved.

Although you're in an optimal position in this aspect of love ability, you can still benefit from a review of strategies for enhancing your skills in the risk-taking area. Particularly if your quiz score was on the low or high end of the risk-evaluator range, you'll want to read the strategies section that addresses the specific approach you can take to maximize the effectiveness of your risking. If you received a low risk-evaluator score or you suspect that you tend to be overly cautious in love, read the section on "Increasing Your Risk-Taking." If, on the other hand, you scored at the high end of the range (and almost placed in the risk-taker category) or you feel you take too many risks in love, turn to the section on "Controlling Your Risk-Taking."

RISK-AVOIDER

Most types of risk-taking are extremely uncomfortable for you. You much prefer to play it safe and not take any chances. Being able to predict and control your life is much more appealing to you than the challenge of dealing with the new or dangerous. Security is what allows you to function best. You find it incredibly stressful to cope with change and uncertainty.

Your aversion to risk-taking has its positive aspects. You can live a very safe life, free from many of the hazards that more adventurous types face. You'll enjoy lifelong friendships within a small, close-knit circle. Far from fickle in your affections, you're happiest with those you've known the longest. You're not one to terminate a relationship easily. You'll do whatever it takes to preserve your relationships, even when the going gets rough. Other people may have a more interesting group of friends and a greater number of friendly acquaintances. But you much prefer to limit your social contacts in scope and number. As far as you're concerned, lots of different personalities can be difficult to contend with. It's easier and safer to cultivate a select group of people you know well and who are similar to you in terms of temperament and background.

In terms of romance, you can only function in a long-term, committed relationship. Whereas the majority of risk-takers are constantly attempting to capture and recapture the initial excitement when two people begin to connect, you much prefer to move past that first stage and remain in the more subdued comfort zone, which can develop only with time. Rather than getting bored in a relationship where you and your partner know everything about each other, you thrive on it. You'd never do anything to jeopardize the security that is associated with a stable relationship. In a world where relationships are constantly breaking up, you make sure yours has staying power.

But lest you become too smug about the positive aspects of being a risk-avoider, consider the disadvantages. Your aversion to taking a chance means that you'll never venture far from what's familiar. You'll remain where it's comfortable because you're unwilling to experience situations that could help you grow. Consequently, you'll deny yourself opportunities to expand your horizons and live the fullest life possible.

In sharp contrast to people who recognize a potential risk but feel it's worthwhile because of the potential gain, you tend to focus on the negatives. Positive thinking is not a skill you've developed to any great extent. When faced with a risk, you don't think you have the abilities to tackle it successfully; instead, you convince yourself that taking a risk is sure to result in disaster. Since you feel this way, even on a subconscious level, it's not surprising that you feel so threatened by what you don't know and can't control.

Your fears can really get the best of you in your love life. Being all too aware that love can be a tremendous risk, you're hesitant to immerse yourself in it totally. Getting involved with someone is a scary prospect for you. If you allow your anxieties to run rampant, you might refrain from ever establishing intimacy. Not being in a love relationship is the only sure way to guarantee that you'll never be hurt.

But even a risk-avoider feels the need to love and be loved.

The fact that you're reading this book now attests to this compelling human urge. Most people who are averse to risking are willing to take a chance on love. But unlike risk-takers or even risk-evaluators, you use every possible precaution to protect yourself and minimize the risks.

You'll be extremely choosy about your partner. While it makes sense to be selective about whom you get involved with, you carry it to an extreme. If you have even the smallest doubt about the person, you resist any involvement. Typically, you look for partners with backgrounds similar to yours who promise a stable life-style. Unfortunately, you lose out on a number of would-be partners who have much to offer and settle instead for someone who seems like a surer bet (even if this person is less intriguing).

Once you finally take the much-deliberated step and get involved, you'll continue to try to play it safe by minimizing your vulnerability. You're likely to guard your emotions and never fully share your feelings with a partner. You'll limit your communication to neutral topics and avoid any troubling is-sues. While you may be together for a long time, the two of you will function more as intimate strangers than as true friends and lovers.

In all probability, you'll never become a risk-taker. It is neither feasible nor desirable to completely reverse your nature. But it is possible for you to become a little more comfortable with risk-taking. You can work toward becoming a risk-evaluator and take a few carefully calculated risks to improve your readiness for love. The section on strategies for "Increasing Your Risk-Taking" will help you do this. But you can't just read this section and then procrastinate. Resolve to take some steps to gradually improve your willingness to take some chances in life and love.

✳ Strategies for More Effective Risking

If you're a risk-taker whose risking may be getting in the way of love, read the section on "Controlling Your Risk-Taking." If you avoid taking risks to the point where you're afraid to take a chance on love, the section on "Increasing Your Risk-Taking" is for you.

CONTROLLING YOUR RISK-TAKING

Taking risks enhances life, even when the outcome isn't exactly the one you hoped for. When you risk, you feel alive. The stimulation keeps you on your toes, ready for more challenges and opportunities.

No one would suggest that you stop taking risks. But you do need to gain some control over your behavior to ensure that those risks you take

- are informed and well planned.
  (You're well aware of the needs behind the risks and the possible consequences, both negative and positive.)
- minimize danger or discomfort to others.
  (Recognizing that any risks you take can affect others, you are careful to avoid inflicting damage or hurt on anyone else, as well as on yourself.)
- emphasize growth over the long-term rather than short-term excitement.
  (You need to focus on risks that have the potential to add something more substantial to your life and your relationship than just a quick thrill.)

You can continue to be a risk-taker without hurting your chances for a successful relationship if you consider these three criteria first. In fact, just expending the time and thought to contemplate a risk instead of immediately pursuing it will help in preventing your risk-taking from damaging your relationship. By critiquing each potential risk, you'll know whether it's worthwhile.

For example, say you have a developing attraction to a member of the opposite sex who is not your partner. The temptation to expand upon what started as a harmless flirtation will be intense if you're bored with your partner. An analysis of the risk of having an affair with the other person might go something like this:

❋   ❋

RISK: Having an affair outside the relationship.

NEED(S) BEHIND THE RISK:
- Alleviating boredom of current sex life.
- Proving attractiveness and sex appeal to someone besides partner.

POSSIBLE POSITIVE CONSEQUENCES OF THE RISK:
- Sexual excitement and fulfillment.
- Discovery that your new lover might be better suited for you than your current partner.

POSSIBLE NEGATIVE CONSEQUENCES OF THE RISK:
- Long-term relationship may break up.
- Partner may become angry and retaliate by being unfaithful.
- Contraction of a sexually transmitted disease.

TO MINIMIZE DANGER OR DISCOMFORT TO OTHERS IF THE RISK IS TAKEN:
- Use safe-sex techniques.
- Take precautions so partner doesn't find out.

GROWTH-PROMOTING ALTERNATIVES TO/ADAPTATIONS OF THE RISK:
- Find ways to add more interest to the sex you share with your partner.

❋   ❋

From this analysis, you may decide that the negative consequences outweigh the positive, especially if you really do care about your partner. You might opt instead for improving your sex life within your current relationship.

There are never any right or wrong answers for this exercise. All you have to do is honestly analyze the dynamics behind each risk you're contemplating. Use the blank worksheet the next time you're considering a risk. Eventually you'll be able to do a mental analysis without putting it on paper.

✳   ✳

RISK: _____

_____

NEED(S) BEHIND THE RISK:

• _____

• _____

POSSIBLE POSITIVE CONSEQUENCES OF THE RISK:

• _____

• _____

POSSIBLE NEGATIVE CONSEQUENCES OF THE RISK:

• _____

• _____

TO MINIMIZE DANGER OR DISCOMFORT TO OTHERS IF THE RISK
IS TAKEN:

• _____

• _____

GROWTH-PROMOTING ALTERNATIVES TO/ADAPTATIONS OF THE
RISK:

• _____

• _____

✳   ✳

In order to take risks without hurting your ability to find
or maintain a love relationship, you'll need to weed out those
which are self-destructive (since you can't expect your partner
to endure the stress of watching you destroy yourself or take
chances which have that potential) or which can cause discomfort or actual loss to your partner. Examples of such destruc-
tive risks include: drug use; smoking; shoplifting; reckless

driving; gambling; having sex without using contraception when the two of you have agreed to prevent pregnancy; jumping from one job to another without ever accruing any benefits; blurting out criticisms and negative comments about your partner without evaluating whether they should be voiced and how our partner will react; infidelity; uncontrolled spending and incurring of debt; risky investments; provoking confrontations; and promoting crisis situations within the relationship simply to add some drama.

But it wouldn't be healthy for you to do away with all risks. For you to be able to love and be loved, you need to be happy with your life. Without an optimal level of risk, you'll be bored, restless, and even depressed.

Look for ways to risk that won't cause major difficulties in your relationship. Find ways to get your adrenaline pumping without involving your partner or compromising his or her security. Alternative forms of excitement can include sports such as sky diving, scuba diving, rock climbing, white water rafting, and motorcycling. Instead of quitting your job to chase a tenuous dream such as acting or writing, you can continue to give your partner the stability of a regular paycheck by remaining in your job while pursuing your interests during your off hours. You can even perform volunteer work (such as working in a soup kitchen or homeless shelter) which benefits your community while affording you some challenging opportunities.

Fill in the next worksheet to reflect your current feelings and plans for risk-taking. Remember to keep your (current or future) partner's needs in mind if you want the relationship to succeed. From time to time, review what you've written and make any changes that are indicated. This monitoring will ensure that you don't compromise your chances for happiness in life and love by too much or too little risk-taking. As you achieve an optimal balance in this area, you'll be enhancing your readiness for love.

---

*   *

_____
DATE

RISKS I'M CURRENTLY TAKING AND WANT TO CONTINUE TAKING:

- *surviving – pursuing choices that benefit me.*
- *Having the ability to move, adapt, fight.*
- _____

RISKS I'M CURRENTLY TAKING AND WANT TO STOP TAKING:

- *Instability – running from and away*
- *If I run + change locations am I*
- *mentally doing the same thing?*

RISKS I'M NOT CURRENTLY TAKING BUT WOULD LIKE TO START TAKING:

- *To give wholly to a relationship*
- *honestly communicating how I feel.*
- *Not to manipulate or potentially doing environment.*

RISKS I'M NOT CURRENTLY TAKING AND DON'T WANT OR INTEND TO TAKE:

- _____
- _____
- _____

*   *

INCREASING YOUR RISK-TAKING

Risk-taking will never be easy for you. You'll probably always have some anxiety when you even contemplate taking a chance. The important thing is not to allow yourself to become immobilized by fear. You need to strive to move beyond your fears so that you can move ahead.

This is especially important in love. In your zeal to protect yourself from becoming too vulnerable, you'll wind up feeling unloved and unloving. If you permit your apprehensions to rule, you may never commit to a relationship. Even when in a committed relationship, you may hold back and never really open up or trust your partner with your thoughts and feelings. You can't be ready for love if you're not ready to risk.

It's imperative that you immediately begin to increase your tolerance for risk. But this doesn't mean that you have to enroll in the nearest hang gliding school or dash to the nearest casino. There are smaller ways you can take risks that don't involve any potential physical or emotional loss. You can live a full life just by taking more emotional and intellectual risks. By gradually letting new ideas and experiences into your life, you'll expand your horizons as well as your willingness to take more risks in the future.

Start off with something as innocuous as trying a new restaurant with an unfamiliar cuisine. Read a new recipe once, file it away, and then attempt to recreate it on your own. Take a drive using back roads instead of major highways and without using a map. Better yet, drive into the country for a weekend without any reservations or plans and see what develops. Enroll in a college course in a field you've never studied.

Once you begin taking small risks and see you're able to withstand the associated stress and uncertainty, you're ready to tackle more substantial ones. At this point, it can be beneficial to try something that involves some physical risk on a controlled basis. You may want to consider spending your next vacation in a program such as Outward Bound, where you're instructed and guided in wilderness experiences. Although participants are well prepared for the challenges of the outdoors, there are no absolute guarantees. By the time the experience is over, the participants' confidence in this ability to tolerate risk and conquer their fears while fending for themselves is dramatically increased. Many individuals who previously attempted to avoid risk in their lives become much more comfortable with risks of all types after one of these experiences. This also holds true for adventure travel such as white water rafting, wagon train trips, or boating experiences where participants help with the sailing. Ask your travel agent for further information.

You probably won't succeed at every risk you take. But you'll discover that the consequences of failing are never quite as worrisome as you had feared. You may not succeed, but you *will* survive. You can learn to be glad that you took each risk because the alternative (stagnation) would have been far worse.

This mindset can be used very effectively in your love relationships. Taking risks in the rest of your life will convince you that you're ready to take a chance on love. Whether it's the initial decision to allow yourself to become involved or the willingness to fully share yourself with your partner, risking can promote growth in your relationship.

There are several different techniques to assist you in your risk-taking quest. Most are simple but effective means of giving you the courage to proceed with risking. Support groups can be extremely helpful, as they put you in touch with other people who are striving to improve their professional or personal lives. A scrapbook composed of newspaper and magazine articles about people who have successfully risked can inspire you to do the same. By assembling and reading this book, you'll be likely to conclude that, if others can take such risks as giving up their jobs to pursue their dreams of sailing around the world or moving to a new city and beginning an entirely different career, you could certainly take a chance on love!

Writing down affirmative statements will help you increase your positive thinking about the worth of risking and your ability to succeed at it. The repetition and action of writing a basic statement such as "I deserve love and it's worth risking" twenty to thirty times a day assists you in ridding yourself of negative thoughts that hold you back.

Similarly, visualizing what you want and seeing yourself getting it can program you for successful risking. By picturing your desired goal in your mind, you'll get a taste of what success and happiness would be like. This will enable you to see that your goal isn't an illusory ideal that can never really be achieved; instead, you'll discover it's attainable and the payback is well worth the effort. But don't confuse visualizing with fantasizing. Fantasy involves unrealistic dreams in which good things happen to you; visualization focuses on realistic imagery that depicts you actively going after what you want and need. Fantasizing doesn't go beyond the imagination, whereas visualizing prepares and energizes for action.

Visualizing love is easy and pleasurable. If you're not currently in a relationship, picture what it would be like to love and be loved. Try to add enough details so you can see and enjoy the activities and feelings associated with loving, but don't become so specific that you'll be setting yourself up for disappointment if some of the details are never realized. You're attempting to develop a scenario that exposes you to the joys of love, not create a rigid image of your partner-to-be. If you get too hung up on extraneous details like height, eye color, or occupation while visualizing, you could find it difficult to accept someone who doesn't possess these characteristics (but is promising in other regards). Concentrate on the warmth and caring you'll experience with your nameless, faceless partner.

If you're already in a relationship but have not yet taken the risks to help it reach its potential, visualizing can also work for you. Picture whatever is currently missing in the relationship (trust, commitment, excitement, intimacy, etc.) and try to make it materialize in your mind. Think of ways the missing ingredient could surface and then enjoy the images of what it would be like to have your life be complete and fulfilling.

To move past the visualizing and put the images into action, commit yourself on paper. Record the specific risk you want or need to take, the reasons why you fear the risk, techniques for cutting your losses if the risk is not paying off, ways to increase your confidence and comfort in taking the risk, and your potential reward(s) for the risk in question. Finally, you'll need to make the ultimate decision: whether or not to take the risk. This can't be a noncommittal response such as "maybe." You need to decide, right on the spot, if you're willing to risk. Being indecisive or procrastinating is guaranteed to lead to no action and, consequently, no attainment of what you want.

An analysis of the risk associated with trying to find love

by getting to know someone could be illustrated as follows. As you can see from this example, the biggest fears were of

---

✳   ✳

THE RISK I WANT/NEED TO TAKE: Trying to connect with a co-worker whom I'm attracted to but hardly know.

MY FEARS ABOUT THIS RISK: I could get rejected and then be embarrassed when I see him at work.

TO CUT MY LOSSES IF THE RISK IS NOT SUCCEEDING, I COULD: Ask him to lunch or for drinks after work, along with some other coworkers so it won't seem so much like a date. I can arrange to receive a phone call at the restaurant and be "called away" so I can escape if it doesn't go well.

I WOULD BE MORE CONFIDENT AND COMFORTABLE ABOUT TAKING THIS RISK IF I: Asked a mutual friend to do some preliminary groundwork (e.g., finding out whether he's involved with anyone and whether he's interested in meeting someone).
Improved my appearance so I'd look and feel more attractive.

MY REWARD(S) FOR THIS RISK-TAKING WOULD BE: Getting to know this person and possibly discovering that we're very compatible.

I CHOOSE TO TAKE THIS RISK:

         ✔__Yes   ____No

✳   ✳

---

rejection and embarrassment. But the possibility of inviting a group of people to lunch or for drinks would make it less of a dating situation and eliminate most of the awkwardness of two people trying to get to know each other under strained circumstances. If the person in question refuses, it can't be construed as a personal rejection, which also minimizes the possibilities for embarrassment. Similarly, if you find that the two of you don't hit it off, it won't be as uncomfortable when there are other people around to keep up the conversation. To increase your comfort level in taking the risk, you might have a mutual friend find out whether he's involved or looking to become involved in a relationship. Your confidence may also be enhanced by making some improvements in your appearance. A reminder of why the risk is worthwhile is the brief but potent statement that something special could develop between the two of you. Obviously, the potential negative consequences of the risk (a little rejection and embarrassment) appear minimal compared to the positive outcome you could enjoy (finding love).

In the next example, the risk of vulnerability remains, but under different circumstances. Here we have a relationship that already exists, but the communication is limited.

✳   ✳

THE RISK I WANT/NEED TO TAKE: To openly share my thoughts and feelings with my partner.

MY FEARS ABOUT THIS RISK: My partner might belittle me and not understand.

TO CUT MY LOSSES IF THE RISK IS NOT SUCCEEDING, I COULD: Stop laying myself on the line and not continue to share my feelings with my partner if they're not accepted.

I WOULD BE MORE CONFIDENT AND COMFORTABLE ABOUT TAKING THIS RISK IF I: Learned more about effective communication by reading some books on the subject.

MY REWARD(S) FOR THIS RISK-TAKING WOULD BE: The possibility of increased emotional intimacy.

I CHOOSE TO TAKE THIS RISK:

___✔ Yes   _____No

✳   ✳

The fear associated with the risk of opening up to your partner is that your feelings may not be understood or accepted. But the realization that you could stop sharing your feelings if they weren't accepted should remind you that you can cut your losses and prevent further pain. Your comfort zone could be increased by reading books on effective communication so you'll feel better prepared to start sharing your thoughts and feelings. The potential reward of increased emotional intimacy appears to be well worth the risk, and it would be foolish not to take the chance.

Use the blank worksheet to perform your own analysis for a risk you'd like to attempt. By being honest about your fears and remembering you can prevent any loss or pain from becoming too overwhelming, you'll be able to take the risks that will enable the love you need and deserve. It won't be easy at first, but you'll quickly find your increased ability to love and be loved is well worth the initial discomfort.

✳   ✳

THE RISK I WANT/NEED TO TAKE: *Trying to connect verbally/intellectually with a guy I know and am totally into.*

MY FEARS ABOUT THIS RISK: *I could be rejected and instead read little reminders that are probably embarrassing.*

TO CUT MY LOSSES IF THE RISK WAS NOT SUCCEEDING, I COULD

_____

_____

_____

I WOULD BE MORE CONFIDENT AND COMFORTABLE ABOUT TAKING THIS RISK IF I: _____

_____

_____

MY REWARD(S) FOR THIS RISK-TAKING WOULD BE:

_____

_____

I CHOOSE TO TAKE THIS RISK:

_____Yes   _____No

✳   ✳

RECOMMENDED READING

Keyes, Ralph. *Chancing It*. Boston: Little, Brown, 1985.
Morscher, Betsy, and Barbara Schindler Jones. *Risk-Taking for Women*. New York: Everest House, 1982.
Viscott, David. *Risking*. New York: Simon & Schuster, 1977.
Weiner, Elliot. *The Ostrich Complex*. New York: Warner, 1986.

→tryy to push too fast.

2

Do You Have Realistic Expectations About Love?

Most of us have at least a little romance in our souls. Even when we encounter problems in our relationships, we retain dreams and hopes about love. When we can, we take the time and effort to make our living and loving as romantic as possible. But few of us can live out our romantic fantasies as fully as we might like.

Too many romantic illusions or expectations can interfere with real love as it's lived outside of song lyrics, romance novels and the silver screen. A realistic attitude that enables you to cope with the ups and downs of love is one of the crucial prerequisites for loving and for being loved.

Find out if you're realistic about love by taking the following quiz. If you discover that you fall short of this important ability, the strategies section will help you arrive at a more realistically positive perspective.

✳   Q U I Z   —   ✳

Find out whether you're ready for love in terms of having realistic expectations for your actual or potential relationship(s). Answer the questions in this two-part quiz honestly, score your answers, and read the profile that corresponds with your total score.

Part I.

   Pick the one answer that best describes your thoughts and feelings on each question.

1. Which is your favorite movie among the following?
   a. *Gone with the Wind*
   b. *When Harry Met Sally . . .*
   c. *Annie Hall*

2. Which best summarizes your philosophy?
   a. You've got to make your own happiness in this world and can't ever depend on anyone else to do it for you.
   b. All I need in my life to be happy is the right person.
   c. To be happy, I need a full and rewarding life, which includes, but is not limited to, the right partner.

3. A good relationship is one in which a couple:
   a. Spends most of their time together.
   b. Allows each other maximum freedom.
   c. Reserves some time to be together but also pursues their individual lives.

4. Your first response when you hear about a young, beautiful woman marrying an older, wealthy man is:
   a. Do they have anything in common?
   b. She's marrying him just for his money.
   c. Lucky her—she found her prince!

5. What's your reaction to television or magazine advertisements that show a couple in an exotic tropical setting absorbed only in each other?
   a. You can't help laughing at Madison Avenue's attempts to sell products by associating them with fairy tale images.

   b. You find yourself envying them and dream of finding that type of love.

   c. You wish you could be enjoying a setting like that with someone you cared about.

6. If you should find or have already found a person who you feel is special but has some undeniable flaws, idiosyncrasies, or problems, you would remind yourself that:

   a. Love will change your partner.

   b. Love is never easy and can often be sheer torture.

   c. You love your partner enough to learn to cope with his or her imperfections.

7. What's the best part about getting married?

   a. Not having to date anymore.

   b. The wedding and honeymoon.

   c. Sharing a life with another person.

8. Your advice to young adults who want to find love:

   a. "Love can be blind, so try to go into it with both eyes wide open and watch out!"

   b. "Know exactly what you want in a partner: looks, occupation, personality, interests."

   c. "Know yourself well and keep an open mind about the type of person who would be good for you."

9. Your preferred reading material is:

   a. Romance or historical novels.

   b. Current fiction.

   c. Nonfiction or humor books.

10. Your advice to friends who are having some marital troubles would be to:

   a. Seek professional counseling or read a self-help book.

   b. Find a good divorce lawyer.

   c. Spend a weekend at a country inn and try to recapture what they had at the beginning of their relationship.

11. Your feelings and response several years ago to the royal wedding of Prince Charles and Lady Di was:

   a. It was a ridiculous media circus; you didn't watch any of it.

   b. It was enchanting; you watched the whole thing.

   c. It was of some historical interest; you watched part of it.

12. Prenuptial contracts are:
  a. Absolutely essential.
  b. Acceptable under some circumstances.
  c. A horrible concept.

13. Growing up, what did you think about your parents' marriage?
  a. Like most of the marriages I saw, it wasn't perfect but I knew my parents loved each other.
  b. It was glamorous, romantic, and the ideal I should strive for.
  c. They were obviously unhappy together and it was a miserable situation for all of us.

Part II.

Answer true or false to each of the following questions. If you're not currently involved in a relationship, answer on the basis of your past relationships and your hopes for a future partner and relationship.

1. I believe in love at first sight. *True*
2. I enjoy doing special things for the person(s) I love and having them be reciprocated, but our schedules only allow this on an infrequent basis. *False*
3. I spend a lot of time daydreaming and thinking about love. *True*
4. The failure and hurt I've experienced in love relationships have made me one of the walking wounded. *True*
5. Even when a couple has a good relationship, it's important for them to have a support system of family and friends. *True*
6. I can be happy with someone who meets 80 percent of my needs and desired characteristics in a partner. *True*
7. It would be impossible for me to find the time or energy for romantic gestures, gift-giving, and events. *False*
8. Only a very few people (with the right looks, personalities, and bank accounts) have any luck in love. *False*
9. I often wish that my partner and I could be alone on a desert island together, free from interference from the outside world. *True*
10. What I want most in a relationship is to be able to be myself. *True*
11. My job, friends, and family will always come first because chances are they'll be in my life longer than any love relationship. *False*
12. I'm convinced there's only one person in the world who's right for me and is my true soulmate. *True False*

13. Love doesn't just magically occur; you have to make it happen. *True*
14. I'd settle for someone who wouldn't bleed me dry (demanding too much time, attention, or money). *False*
15. I'm not very optimistic about having a successful long-term relationship, especially when I hear that almost one in two marriages ends in divorce. *False*
16. My current (or most recent) relationship has had its ups and downs, but I've been happy the majority of the time. *True*
17. I need constant confirmation of my partner's love.
18. It's extremely important to me to have a very attractive partner. *True*

SCORING

Part I. Total up your points as follows.

	a	b	c
1.	a- 5	b- 3	c- 1
2.	a- 1	b- 5	c- 3
3.	a- 5	b- 1	c- 3
4.	a- 3	b- 1	c- 5
5.	a- 1	b- 5	c- 3
6.	a- 5	b- 1	c- 3
7.	a- 1	b- 5	c- 3
8.	a- 1	b- 5	c- 3
9.	a- 5	b- 3	c- 1
10.	a- 3	b- 1	c- 5
11.	a- 1	b- 5	c- 3
12.	a- 1	b- 3	c- 5
13.	a- 3	b- 5	c- 1

Part II. Take the total you earned in Part I and, for each question you answered true, add or subtract points as follows:

If you answered true for 1, 3, 9, 12, 17 or 18—add five points for each answer.

If you answered true for 4, 7, 8, 11, 14 or 15—subtract one point for each answer.

The total is your score for the quiz. Find which range your score fell in.

- 55 to 95—Romantic *64*
33 to 54—Realistic
7 to 32—Cynical

✳ Profiles

Find the profile that corresponds to your quiz score.

ROMANTIC

With all the romantic greeting cards, clothes, home furnishings, music, movies, books, restaurants and vacations available, it should be easy to add enough romance to your life so that you get your daily dose of "Vitamin R." Unfortunately, it's not quite as simple as it might appear. There may be a lot of resources for putting more romance in your life, but many of them turn out to be mere props and accessories that add only a superficial smattering of the romance you crave. The other problem is that, as a true romantic, you probably have an insatiable need for romance. No matter how much of it you get, it's never enough. You try to cram as many romantic illusions as you can into your life, but it can be a constant battle to keep reality from intruding into your fantasy world.

Your romanticism may have developed from a number of sources. Perhaps you've sat through too many old movies and internalized what you saw on the screen. Instead of seeing examples of real love in action around you, you may have focused on the hundred or so minutes of intense passion and sweeping romance that Omar Sharif and Julie Christie or Humphrey Bogart and Ingrid Bergman provided. Romance novels can also be a culprit if you decide that you must have that same level of adventure and glamour in your own life. Although the characters, settings and situations are purely fictional, you may have convinced yourself that you can recreate similar scenarios in the three-dimensional world you live in.

Your childhood experiences may also have played a significant role in making you a romantic. If your parents carefully created the illusion of a fairy tale marriage, you grew up thinking these romantic images were what love was all about. You may never have been exposed to the realities and inner workings of an intimate relationship, or maybe you never noticed them because your attention was focused on the trappings of romance. Lavish gifts, elegant entertaining, a beau-

tiful home and exquisite clothes and jewelry may say something about a life-style, but it does not begin to reveal
anything about the love between two people. If you know more
about what your parents owned or did than how they thought
and felt as individuals and as a couple, you may be in danger of
emphasizing the superficial aspects of relationships over the
more substantial elements like communication, compatibility
and caring.

On the other hand, you may have been raised in a home
that lacked romance or even love. You may be the product of a
broken marriage. Even if your parents were together, life
might have been difficult. There may have been little time,
energy or money for anything other than basic survival. As a
result, you may have dreamed about finding the romance that
would make your life dramatically different from the one your
parents endured.

Other causative factors might include a perfectionistic
streak (where only the absolute best will suffice), low self-
esteem (which can only be increased by having a highly desirable partner and a glamorous life-style), or a sense of entitle-
ment (where you believe that you deserve the ultimate that life
and love can offer). It might even be due to a subconscious
desire to avoid love; as long as you can convince yourself that
anything less than the romantic ideal is not worth settling for,
you can put off getting involved in a real relationship.

Whatever the reason behind your preoccupation with romance, it appears likely that you've allowed it to escalate to
unmanageable proportions. Romance is certainly an enriching
ingredient in a relationship, but you tend to focus on it as *the*
major element in love. Your lack of a realistic perspective on
love will lead to many disappointments when your unattain-
able expectations aren't met.

The search for a suitable partner is difficult for anyone, but
it's close to impossible for you to find the right person. Your
requirements for a mate may be so stringent that you'll never
feel anyone comes close to meeting them. You may feel your
ability to delineate specifics about what you want in a partner
(e.g., appearance, occupation, family background) will help
you discover that special someone, but in reality all it does is

weed out every potential lover who doesn't meet your criteria. You're probably much more successful in eliminating possible partners from your life than you are in bringing any promising candidates into your life. Waiting for that one perfect individual who can fulfill your romantic fantasies can be a very lengthy proposition. Some people go a lifetime without love because they're unable to find anyone who meets their romantic ideal.

But it's also possible that, as a romantic, you have an active dating life (either currently or in the past). The courtship stage is the one that pleases you the most, so you may be quite happy being perpetually at this entry level of love. It's the later stages of intimate, mature love that leave you scared or unsatisfied, so you're an expert at making sure your relationships never get to that point. Instead, you find yourself caught up in the mystery and excitement of getting to know someone. You love the romance that's so prevalent at this stage, with both you and your partner always careful to present yourselves at your best. Since you're still trying to prove yourselves to each other and to establish a relationship, you work extremely hard to make everything in your life together as special as it can be.

But inevitably, as you get to know someone well, some of the illusions will fade. Because pretenses can't be kept up indefinitely, you'll eventually discover things about your partner that will shatter his or her image of perfection. Your romantic escapades will start to decrease in frequency and intensity. Whereas a realist can accept the lessening of the initial passion and enjoy the deepening of real intimacy, you as a romantic cannot. Since you're not about to settle for a routine love relationship, there's only one choice: move on to the next partner. And the next, and the next after that . . . as you continue your endless quest for nonstop romance.

This is not to imply that romantics never commit to marriage or long-term relationships. Any one or a combination of factors may influence you finally to settle down. You may have a whirlwind courtship and quick engagement that offer plenty of romance. Marriage may occur before you really get to know each other, warts and all. Or your family may pressure you into marriage. You may also find that satisfying other needs (e.g., security) is proving to be even stronger than your longing for romance.

Once you're in a committed relationship, you may stick with it because of your religious convictions, concerns for your family, or lack of opportunity to find a partner you'd be happier with. But remaining in a relationship and being happy in it are two entirely different things. You're likely to enjoy fantasizing about your ideal partner more than actually being with your mate. Because reality never lives up to your expectations, you may tend to avoid taking action to improve your real life and love. Instead of making the most of your relationship, you escape to novels, movies, music, and other means of simulating the romance that's so important to you.

If you're a hard-core romance addict, you may be unwilling to give up or sublimate any part of your dreams or illusions. Stubbornly, you may insist on intense and continual romance in your life, regardless of the cost. Since your partner falls short of your romantic ideal, you never fail to make him or her over in the image you'd prefer. You may make excessive demands on your partner to be romantic, ignoring the fact that the most romantic gestures and words lose something when the giver has been ordered to produce them on command. In your relentless obsession with making and keeping romance in your life, you may place more emphasis on the superficial aspects of loving and fail to communicate with your loved one about what he or she thinks and feels. Small wonder then if your partner becomes unhappy in the relationship!

You don't have to give up your romanticism completely to be ready for love. (A little romance can actually do quite a lot for a relationship.) All you have to do is temper it with a slightly more realistic perspective on love. You can learn how in the strategies section of this chapter by reading about "Becoming More Realistic About Love."

REALISTIC

Although it may not always seem like it, you've got the best of both worlds. Your realistic nature permits you to be romantic at some times and cynical at others. When love goes wrong, you may wish you were more of a cynic in the hope that a more caustic view of love would keep the hurt from getting too bad. When things go well in a relationship, you might berate yourself for not being more of a romantic. But ultimately, only a realist is really ready for love. Your falling between the two extremes of romanticism and cynicism puts you in an ideal place to love and be loved.

As a realist, chances are you grew up in a well-adjusted family where your parents were basically happy with each other and their life together. You saw that love wasn't always perfect, but weren't bothered by it because the good seemed to outweigh the bad. When you started a love life of your own, you probably experienced some ups and downs, but you've managed to find a comfortable middle ground where you can enjoy the realities of love without the burdens of too much romanticism or cynicism.

But don't kid yourself into believing you'll never again have to give any thought to whether you're realistic about love, after you finish reading this section. As people and circumstances in your life change, so may your perspective. Just because you've been a realist for years doesn't mean you'll stay one for the rest of your life. Every so often you need to monitor your level of realism and make sure you're not becoming more romantic or cynical than you should be. Should you ever find you're deviating from realism, you can refer back to the strategies section on "Becoming More Realistic About Love" (if you're leaning toward romanticism) or "Becoming a Little More Romantic" (to ward off excessive cynicism). You'll also want to check "Becoming More Realistic About Love" if you scored at the high end of the realistic range, or "Becoming a Little More Romantic" if you scored at the low end of the realistic range.

CYNICAL

You might disagree with being called cynical. As far as you're concerned, you're just being realistic. You're well aware there are no guarantees in love and you want to make sure you land on your feet when something goes wrong. You find nothing wrong with your cautious approach, condoning it as simple self-protection. And, of course, there *isn't* anything wrong with looking out for yourself and going through life with both eyes open. But when you continually harbor doubts that love can work, you create a self-fulfilling prophecy in which your skepticism prevents you from finding joy in love and making your relationship successful. At best, you end up doing nothing to promote a loving relationship; at worst, you actively sabotage any chances of happiness with a partner.

The roots of this cynicism can usually be traced either to a major hurt you experienced in your love life or to subtle parental messages you received while growing up. The most obvious cause is a past relationship that didn't work out. If you cared very deeply for someone and were later mistreated in some way by this person, the experience could have soured your perspective on love. Being neglected, rejected, or abused by your loved one is extremely traumatic. All it takes is one incident to make you wary about love. If you've had a series of negative romantic experiences, you're even more likely to develop a jaundiced view of love.

You may also have been exposed to cynical attitudes about love during your childhood. If your parents were unhappy with each other, you were probably aware of their dissatisfaction. Whether your parents suffered silently or voiced feelings of bitterness or regret about their relationship, it would be diffi-cult not to be affected by their experiences and emotions. Instead of perceiving love and marriage as something desir-able, you may have learned to see it as something to be endured when necessary or avoided if possible.

Once you become cynical about love, it quickly evolves into a self-perpetuating tendency. You'll find no shortage of rea-sons to justify your negativity. Every time you hear about a failed relationship, you nod your head knowingly and chalk it up to yet another instance where love didn't work. You'll smugly remind yourself that you're too smart to let that happen to you. You're proud you're not a starry-eyed romantic who expects the best from love and then winds up getting hurt. When confronted with a successful relationship, you'll try to deny all the positives and will search instead for the problems that you're convinced lurk under the surface. No matter how stable or happy two people seem together, you don't buy it because you feel it's impossible for love to go that well. After all, this is real life, not a fairy tale.

As a cynic, you may avoid love completely and never get involved in a relationship. This ensures you won't get hurt or experience any kind of a loss from a failed relationship; you can't ever lose what you never had. Going through life without love may have its drawbacks, but it does enable you to concentrate your energies on other areas (such as work) since you won't have to spend time nursing your wounds from the battles of love. You can enjoy a wide circle of friends of both sexes while escaping romantic involvement with any of them. While you won't experience the heady rush of falling in love or the warm reassurance that accompanies a long-term relationship, you'll be spared the disappointment of love turning out all wrong.

But even a cynic can succumb to Cupid's arrow. The fact that you're reading this book shows you do have some interest in loving and being loved. This may stem from familial or societal pressure to settle down, as most of us are still expected to be part of a couple and find it difficult to function solo on a permanent basis. You may get involved in a relationship for reasons as unromantic as enhancing your career (some employers tend to hire and promote married candidates over singles) or providing safe sex (AIDS has encouraged monogamous relationships). Maybe your motive is escape from the perils of the dating scene, which can be even scarier than maintaining an intimate relationship. Perhaps you've had problems dealing with loneliness and simply want to feel more connected.

Beginning a relationship is never easy, but it's doubly difficult for you. Your distrust of love makes you suspicious of every potential partner who comes along. You look for the hidden agendas of people who seem interested in you, never accepting their words or actions at face value. You try not to let your guard down even momentarily; that would make you vulnerable, and you're not about to let that happen. Even when someone's intentions appear honorable, you continue to have doubts. A multitude of questions and concerns torment you and effectively prevent you from enjoying the affections bestowed upon you. Because you just can't be sure things will work out, you opt for safety rather than passion. By holding back, you control intimacy and involvement at nonthreatening levels. When a relationship appears to have potential for real closeness, you're likely to withdraw.

If a persistent suitor manages to break through some of your barriers, it's possible for you to have a long-term relationship. Unlike a romantic who, convinced that true love lies just around the corner, will pursue one relationship after another to find that special love, your cynical nature precludes any such illusions and hopes. Although you may not be entirely happy with one partner, you feel there would be little point in getting involved with someone else. You philosophize that a different relationship would just bring different problems, so you stick with what you have.

Longevity in a relationship can be impressive, but only when both partners are satisfied. It's pointless to stay in a relationship that doesn't meet your needs. You only succeed in denying yourself and your partner the ultimate rewards love can offer. But to reap these benefits, you need to recognize and accept that love *can* work. Turn to the strategies section on "Becoming Less Cynical About Love."

✳ Strategies for a More Realistic Approach to Love

The first section, "Becoming More Realistic About Love," is for you if you're a romantic. "Becoming Less Cynical About Love" is your section if the quiz revealed that you have cynical views about love.

BECOMING MORE REALISTIC ABOUT LOVE

Dreams, hopes, and fantasies can enhance our lives. They can relieve the tedium of day-to-day existence and give us something to strive toward. They enlarge and expand the possibilities that are readily available, providing us with the vision of something better than what we currently have. Without them, we might never recognize what could be or try to attain the utmost that life can offer.

But none of these things are reality. Most of us understand and accept this. We're fully aware of a distinct demarcation between what we wish for and what's realistically possible. Because we don't expect our dreams and fantasies to be completely realized, we enjoy reality even when it falls short of our ideal and work hard at making the most of whatever life offers.

As a romantic, relinquishing dreams is extremely difficult for you. You have a definite image of what should be and don't want anything less than the ideal. You feel that you'd be selling yourself short by making do with things and people that aren't perfect.

While you may romanticize other areas of your life, love is probably the area that harbors most of your romantic illusions. You know exactly what you expect from love and you won't settle for what you'd consider a watered-down version.

You can continue to hold on zealously to your cherished beliefs and dreams if they make you happy. But chances are they cause more misery than satisfaction. The likelihood of your living out your fantasies is extremely remote. In the real world where love partners all possess human flaws and shortcomings, there is no romantic perfection to be found. As you continue to experience one disappointment after another, the pursuit of your romantic ideal may give you pain instead of pleasure.

Since the collision of reality with fantasy causes you discomfort, you may opt for living exclusively in a dream world where reality is not allowed to intrude. You can escape into the fantasies offered by romantic novels and movies, while refusing to let real love with its unavoidable blemishes into your life. But the satisfaction provided by romantic illusions can be short-lived and unsatisfying. True and lasting happiness demands that you become more realistic about love.

You won't be required to abandon all your dreams and fantasies, but to use them to supplement real life rather than substitute for it. You can certainly spice up a relationship from time to time, and through the occasional use of props and illusions that add some variety and glamour to reality, you can make things more special for both you and your partner.

Romantic settings, games, costumes, gifts, and music are all acceptable additions to your love life. It's your unrealistic, overly romantic *expectations* that need to be toned down.

While you can argue that the only way to get the best is to expect it, you need to recognize you've gone beyond merely expecting the best that love can realistically offer. You've carried it to an extreme by expecting the ultimate relationship, conjured up in your dreams and fantasies. You shouldn't become a cynic and expect the worst, but you do need to come to terms with the realities of love.

If your romanticism has prevented you from finding love or being happy in a relationship, you must take some time now to realize how unrealistic your expectations for a potential partner and an actual relationship have been. It may be difficult at first, but you'll have to revise your requirements so they become more attainable. The worksheets that follow will help you do this. After you read the examples, you can fill out your own.

✳   ✳

WHAT I'VE BEEN EXPECTING: To find someone with a movie star's face, an athlete's body, a millionaire's bank account, a dancer's grace, an artist's sensitivity, a college professor's intellect, and a comedian's sense of humor, all in one neat package.

THE REALITY OF GETTING IT: Slim to none. In twenty years of looking, I still haven't found this person!

BARRIER(S) TO GETTING IT: This person doesn't seem to exist in real life, only in my imagination.

HOW IT HURTS ME TO CONTINUE EXPECTING THIS: I go through life without love because I haven't been willing to consider anyone who falls short of these requirements.

WHAT I CAN REALISTICALLY GET AND ENJOY: A partner who's intelligent, reasonably good-looking, personable, and caring.

WHAT I CAN DO TO GET IT: Stop ruling out people who don't meet my unrealistic requirements; begin to meet and date more people.

✳   ✳

This example illustrates an overly romantic and unsuccessful search for the perfect love partner. Expecting and demanding that a potential partner be the ideal man or woman is unrealistic and will ultimately prove fruitless. A novel or movie may contain this paragon of virtue, but he or she is only a fictional character. This person cannot be found in real life, as years of looking for him or her have probably revealed. Until this unrealistic expectation is given up, the joy of real love will never be known. If this person never comes along (which is 99.9 percent likely), love with an available man or woman will have been postponed for years, or possibly even a lifetime. By revising the original expectations while still delineating fairly high standards for a partner, the chances of finding love are enhanced. All it takes is a willingness to know and accept people who may not be perfect but still have a lot to offer!

✳   ✳

WHAT I'VE BEEN EXPECTING: The earth to move when I have sex with a new partner.

THE REALITY OF GETTING IT: I've read about it happening, but it's escaped me so far and I don't know how to make it happen.

BARRIER(S) TO GETTING IT: I don't speak up and let my partners know what I like; I want it to happen spontaneously since that's more romantic.

HOW IT HURTS ME TO CONTINUE TO EXPECT THIS: I'm always disappointed and lose interest in every partner. I'm always moving on to the next one in the hope of finding perfect sex.

WHAT I CAN REALISTICALLY GET AND ENJOY: Sex that provides pleasure for both me and a partner I care about.

WHAT I CAN DO TO GET IT: Give a new partner and a relationship a chance to develop over time. I need to realize that the first time won't be as satisfying as what could happen with more practice and deeper emotional ties.

✳   ✳

The quest here for perfect sex (as a prime ingredient of perfect love) is preventing a relationship from ever developing. The unrealistic expectation that an intense orgasm must occur when having sex for the first time with a new partner is likely to result in severe disappointment when it doesn't happen. This can lead to discarding one new partner after another in an attempt to experience immediate fireworks rather than taking the time to develop the communication and caring that's necessary for great sex. By recognizing that sex can be satisfying even if the ultimate doesn't happen immediately, there's an increased possibility of attaining sexual compatibility with that person.

✳   ✳

WHAT I'VE BEEN EXPECTING: Nonstop romance and passion in a long-term relationship.

THE REALITY OF GETTING IT: Seems to be less and less as time goes on.

BARRIER(S) TO GETTING IT: The initial excitement of falling in love has long faded. Both of us are short on the time and energy needed for romance.

HOW IT HURTS ME TO CONTINUE TO EXPECT THIS: I become overly critical of my partner and our relationship. Sometimes I even toy with the idea of breaking up so I can find real romance.

WHAT I CAN REALISTICALLY GET AND ENJOY: Real love, as well as occasional romantic gestures and interludes with my partner.

WHAT I CAN DO TO GET IT: Focus on the positives of our relationship. Stop expecting a fairy-tale romance to occur in real life, but still add some romance to our lives every so often.

✳   ✳

Unlike the first two worksheets, which focused on problems relating to finding love and the "right" partner, this third worksheet addresses an established relationship. The perceived problem is unrealistically expecting the same intensity of passion in the long term as was experienced in the initial days of the relationship. While even relationships of many years can be romantic, few maintain the same degree of fever as when love was just beginning. Instead, love deepens and matures, replacing such heady excitement with more meaningful caring and commitment. This development in a relationship has to be understood and accepted. It should not be threatening or depressing. Mourning the inevitable loss of the early passion is harmful for your relationship as it stands now.

Now it's your turn to fill out a worksheet. Be ruthlessly honest in recording your expectations about love and the reality of having these expectations realized. Be as creative and positive as possible when revising your expectations. You're not trying to deprive yourself of the good things associated with love, so don't settle for too little. But you do want to be realistic and write down achievable goals and expectations. In doing so, you'll be embracing reality rather than running away from it. You'll be able to find and enjoy *real* love instead of just a facade that looks good on the surface but has no real depth or meaning.

✳   ✳

WHAT I'VE BEEN EXPECTING: _____

_____

_____

THE REALITY OF GETTING IT: _____

_____

_____

BARRIER(S) TO GETTING IT: _____

_____

_____

HOW IT HURTS ME TO CONTINUE TO EXPECT THIS: _____

_____

_____

WHAT I CAN REALISTICALLY GET AND ENJOY: _____

_____

_____

WHAT I CAN DO TO GET IT: _____

_____

_____

_____

✳   ✳

BECOMING LESS CYNICAL ABOUT LOVE

Cynicism can be difficult to overcome. Once you start seeing life and love in a negative way, you'll find unlimited opportunities to reinforce these attitudes. Things *do* go wrong and you often have little control over preventing the unwanted from occurring. This serves to convince you that your cynicism is warranted and necessary for survival.

But you may not be quite as successful in convincing yourself that you're happy. While your cynical perspective goes a long way in guarding against letting loose with your emotions and getting hurt later, it diminishes your emotional investment in a relationship and therefore limits the rewards you can receive from loving and being loved. Being wary about other people's motives, you'll make sure you don't get involved with the wrong people. The trouble is you may have inadvertently ruled out some of the right ones, because your carefulness in avoiding the negative consequences of love isn't matched by equal care in facilitating the positive aspects of love. Your negative focus substantially interferes with your love ability.

Obviously, you can't just will yourself to become less cynical. It will take some time and energy to develop a different perspective on love. You'll need to devote a lot of your attention to the ways you allow your thoughts to become distorted. Once you recognize these distortions, you can work on revising your thinking to reflect a more positive and realistic approach.

Psychologists who specialize in cognitive therapy have delineated numerous types of thought distortions. There are six of them that appear to contribute heavily to cynicism. Although they tend to occur automatically, you can learn to revise your perceptions and formulate a more rational response.

Discarding the positive/tunnel vision

Most everything has both positive and negative aspects. But as a cynic, you may have developed a mental filter, which collects negative thoughts while getting rid of positive ones.

EXAMPLE:
"One of every two marriages ends in divorce, so why even bother to get married?"
Revised thought:
"If one of every two marriages fails, that means the other succeeds. It may be a fifty-fifty gamble, but it's worth it."

EXAMPLE:
"Our relationship has lost most of its excitement. It now seems very predictable and ordinary."
Revised thought:
"Some of the initial excitement has faded, but we've developed a comfortable intimacy that is rewarding in its own right."

Fortune-telling

There's no way of knowing exactly what the future holds. Only a cynic is convinced it is possible to predict what is to come. And, of course, the future a cynic predicts is always negative.

EXAMPLE:
"There's no point in going out with her; it'll never work out."

Revised thought:
"After spending a little time with her, I'll be in a better position to know whether she's right for me."

EXAMPLE:
"Our relationship is good now, but I doubt it will stay that way."
Revised thought:
"No one ever knows what will happen in the future, but I can take steps to keep the relationship healthy."

Mind reading

Closely related to fortune-telling, mind reading is another impossibility. Except in science fiction, no one can know what someone else is really thinking. A cynic may tend to ignore this fact and decide that he or she knows exactly what's on other people's minds.

EXAMPLE:
"I can tell she's not interested in me."
Revised thought:
"The only way I'll know for sure whether she wants to go out with me is to ask her."

EXAMPLE:
"He didn't care about what I wanted."
Revised thought:
"My needs and desires were sometimes ignored because I allowed them to be. Maybe if I had better communicated what I wanted, he would have behaved differently."

Magnification

When problems occur, the best way to deal with them is head on. As calmly as possible, you need to face the fact that a problem exists and then take action to make things better. But you may irrationally distort the severity of the difficulty and convince yourself it's a major catastrophe that you can't handle.

EXAMPLE:
"If I ask her out and she says no, I'll be so embarrassed that I'll never be able to face her again at work."
Revised thought:
"Even if she chooses not to go out with me, she'd probably be flattered that I asked and we could remain on friendly terms with each other."

EXAMPLE:
"Once a couple's sex life starts deteriorating, that's a sure sign of impending doom for their relationship."
Revised thought:
"A couple's sex life has its natural highs and lows, but this doesn't have to be a major problem if they really care about each other."

All-or-nothing thinking

Most things in life are not absolute. There's an infinite number of variations and gradations, both subtle and marked, which makes it impossible to expect people and situations always to be one exact way. But as a cynic, you probably tend to see things in black or white instead of all the possible shades of gray.

EXAMPLE:
"I've never done well in love."
Revised thought:
"I've had my share of disappointments in love, but I've had some happy experiences as well."

EXAMPLE:
"It's impossible to meet anyone decent."
Revised thought:
"Meeting the right person isn't easy, but my chances will be dramatically improved if I make an attempt to meet lots of different people."

Overgeneralization

A scientist would never formulate any conclusions on a single event. But that's exactly what a cynic does when he or she overgeneralizes. One isolated negative occurrence is seen as an invariable pattern.

EXAMPLE:
"I never meet anyone at parties, so why bother going?"
Revised thought:
"I didn't have much luck at the last party I went to, but there're bound to be different people at the next one. It's probably worth my while to go to most of the parties I'm invited to."

EXAMPLE:
"You can't trust good-looking men."
Revised thought:
"I had a bad experience with one man who was very attractive, but I do have some friends who have good relationships with great-looking guys."

Reading and filling out the following worksheet will enable you to identify your negative thoughts and distortions. In addition to formulating a revised thought, there's also a space to identify the benefits of the new thought. This is followed by a space for creating a safety guard to protect you from the initial anxiety that will accompany a change in thought patterns. As a cynic, you've developed a way of thinking that has become comfortable (although ultimately unfulfilling). To develop more realistic and positive thoughts that will empower love, it's important for you to be aware of the benefits of revising your thoughts and to understand that you can limit your vulnerability. You don't have to become overly idealistic and romantic about love; you can take measures to protect yourself while opening up to love.

The examples on the worksheets are self-explanatory. Use the blank one to work on your own thoughts about finding and keeping love. The progress you make in decreasing your cynicism will have a direct bearing on your ability to love and be loved, both now and in the future.

❋   ❋

NEGATIVE THOUGHT: Blind dates are likely to be awkward or boring. They're a waste of time.

TYPE OF DISTORTION(S): Discarding the positive/tunnel vision.

REVISED THOUGHT: Even if things don't work out romantically with a blind date, I can still enjoy going to a nice restaurant and movie.

BENEFITS OF REVISED THOUGHT: Increased number of dates and opportunities to meet someone special.

SAFETY GUARD: Being selective about which blind dates I accept. I'll only accept those offered by people who really know me and understand what I'm looking for.

❋   ❋

❋   ❋

NEGATIVE THOUGHT: He never loved me.

TYPE OF DISTORTION(S): Mind-reading. All-or-nothing thinking.

REVISED THOUGHT: He told me he loved me and some of his actions seemed to indicate this. He wasn't able to give me everything I needed, but I do feel he tried to love me in his own way.

BENEFITS OF REVISED THOUGHT: Decreased bitterness and resentment about a relationship that didn't work out; increased willingness to take a chance on a new relationship.

SAFETY GUARD: Choosing my partner carefully to make sure my love is reciprocated. I'll only get involved with someone who can love me in a whole and healthy way, and isn't afraid to show it.

❋   ❋

✳

NEGATIVE THOUGHT: _____

_____

TYPE OF DISTORTION(S): _____

_____

REVISED THOUGHT: _____

_____

_____

BENEFITS OF REVISED THOUGHT: _____

_____

SAFETY GUARD: _____

_____

_____

✳

RECOMMENDED READING

Beck, Aaron T. *Love Is Never Enough*. San Francisco: Harper & Row, 1988.

Burns, David D. *Intimate Connections*. New York: Morrow, 1985.

Cassell, Carol. *Swept Away: Why Women Fear Their Own Sexuality*. New York: Simon & Schuster, 1984.

Diamond, Jed. *Looking for Love in All the Wrong Places*. New York: Putnam, 1988.

Earle, Ralph, and Meltsner, Susan. *Come Here/Go Away: Stop Running from the Love You Want*. New York: Pocket Books, 1991.

Hindy, Carl C., Archie Brodsky, and J. Conrad Schwartz. *If This Is Love, Why Do I Feel So Insecure?* New York: Atlantic Monthly Press, 1985.

Katz, Stan J., and Aimee E. Liu. *False Love and Other Romantic Illusions*. New York: Ticknor & Fields, 1988.

Schaef, Anne Wilson. *Escape From Intimacy*. San Francisco: Harper & Row, 1989.

Schaeffer, Brenda. *Is It Love Or Is It Addiction?* New York: Harper/Hazelden, 1987.

Tennov, Dorothy. *Love and Limerance*. New York: Stein & Day, 1978.

3

* **3** *

Are You Able to Make and Keep a Commitment to Love?

Falling in love is usually the easy part. Staying in love can be much harder. Maintaining a relationship after the initial thrill diminishes can be difficult. Unless you're willing to make a commitment to keep your relationship growing, love can falter or die when problems occur.

Love and life inevitably contain disappointment and disillusionment. When things don't go the way you wanted them to, you might be tempted to escape from the situation. Relationships can fall apart fairly easily, whereas coping with change and adversity requires substantial effort.

But ending a relationship that is experiencing problems may not be much of a solution. You'll no doubt encounter a similar set of problems with your next romantic involvement. By abandoning a relationship in distress, you'll be losing out on the satisfaction of achieving a long-term love that has survived numerous challenges.

Trying to make love work can be far more rewarding than giving up on it. But it does require faith, trust, flexibility, and a real commitment. The quiz that follows will help you discover whether you're capable of this. Then read the strategies sec-

---

* Q U I Z *

Choose the response that best reflects what you'd be most likely to do in each situation.

1. You buy some shares of stock on your broker's advice, intending to hold it for several years. Although the stock has done well over the past twenty years, it has been declining ever since you bought it. The company is currently experiencing some organizational changes and predicts that profits will be up again within the year. What do you do?
   a. Nothing. Your plans were to hold it for a few years and you don't see any reason to alter those plans.
   b. Sell the stock immediately. You'll lose some money by selling at the current lower price but you'd rather cut your losses before you get any worse.
   c. Monitor the stock and company. You'll hold on to the stock but will watch it carefully to make sure things get back on track within the predicted time period; if they don't, you'll consider selling it after discussion with your broker.

2. A friend has highly recommended a movie that has just come out on video. You generally respect her opinion, although there have been a few films that you disagreed about. You rent the video and start watching it but find you're not enjoying it. After ten minutes, what do you do?
   a. Stop watching it. Your time is too valuable to waste on films that aren't good.
   b. Continue to watch the movie until the end. After all, you paid three dollars to rent the movie and set aside a couple of hours to watch it.
   c. Give it another fifteen minutes. If you still can't get into it, you can return it and find something you'll like better.

3. There's a restaurant you've eaten at regularly for the past year. The food has always been good and the restaurant is fairly close to your

home. But when you go there this week, the food and service aren't up to their usual quality. Will you go back again?

 a. Probably. You'd like to give it another chance since all restaurants occasionally have an off night.

 b. Never. You've already had one bad meal there, so why go back for more?

 c. Definitely. Another restaurant could be even worse.

4. When you hear that a couple in their seventies are getting a divorce after fifty-plus years of marriage, what's your reaction?

 a. It's too bad they waited so long; they were probably unhappy for years.

 b. If there were problems with the marriage, there was no point in continuing it; you're never too old to want and deserve happiness.

 c. If they stayed together that long, it's ridiculous to end it at this stage; surely they could make the best of it in their old age.

5. For Christmas, a friend gives you a certificate for a personal color analysis. You've never had it done before, so you take advantage of the opportunity. You're shocked to learn that your favorite color (which dominates your whole wardrobe) is all wrong for you. What do you do now?

 a. Continue to wear the clothes you have, but also buy some new outfits and accessories in the recommended color scheme.

 b. Stick with your old clothes; it's ludicrous to invest in a new wardrobe and change your image just because a color analyst said you're not wearing the right color.

 c. Go on a shopping spree and buy all new things.

6. You've always been committed to physical fitness, but your physician has just diagnosed an orthopedic problem with your feet. Running (which you love) would aggravate the condition. Which decision would you be most likely to make?

 a. Continue running. Nothing is ever 100 percent safe.

 b. Stop all physical activities and take up chess instead.

 c. Switch to a sport such as swimming that is less stressful to your feet.

7. You've been promoted or transferred to a new city. While you've always lived in a single family house and would like to continue to do so, you're uneasy about the current mortgage rates, which

would make your monthly payments extremely high. What's your next step?

   a. Buy a condo right away and forget about a house.

   b. Rent a house, save your money, and make a move to buy a house when rates come down.

   c. Buy a house immediately and pray every month you'll be able to meet the mortgage payments.

8. For several years it's been a tradition for you to cook Thanksgiving dinner for friends and family. This year, however, your job has been extremely demanding and you'll probably have to spend a few hours working on Thanksgiving. How do you handle turkey day?

   a. Still cook dinner even though it would be incredibly stressful to worry about both work and a big party.

   b. Declare a moratorium on Thanksgiving, inform family and friends that you won't be celebrating and microwave a frozen turkey dinner for yourself while working.

   c. Ask everyone to bring a dish so all you have to do is roast the turkey, thus giving you enough time to cram a few hours of work in without too much hassle.

9. You've been fairly happy in your work, but you've become aware that opportunities in your field will be diminishing in the upcoming years. What will you do?

   a. Stick with your job and ignore predictions about the future. If you switched fields now, you'd waste all those years of experience and training.

   b. Apply for entry-level positions in fields that are targeted for high growth in the future. You don't want to miss out on the hot prospects in the years to come.

   c. Continue with your current job, but keep your eyes open for new possibilities and consider enrolling in school part-time to get some training. You're in no hurry to change your line of work, but you want to be realistic and keep your options open.

10. After making arrangements to go out to dinner with a friend you haven't seen in a while, you get invited to a party on that same night. The party sounds fabulous, but you know your friend is looking forward to your getting together. Do you accept the invitation?

   a. Yes, provided your friend can also come and would like to attend the party. If not, you would forget about the party.

b. No. You stick to your original plans and keep the dinner date with your friend.

c. Yes. The party is too good to miss. There will be plenty of other occasions where the two of you can get together.

11. A food product that you've always enjoyed was shown to cause cancer in laboratory rats. To use or not to use?

  a. Stop using it immediately. You can't be too careful.

  b. Use it cautiously, limiting its use and keeping up with new developments. If further studies conclusively show an increased risk of cancer, you'll stop using it.

  c. Continue to use it because this was only the first study on the subject, and it tested animals rather than humans. Everything seems to cause cancer, anyway, so there's no point in worrying about it.

12. A charity you've made regular contributions to has been accused of misusing its funds. An investigation is pending. What do you do?

  a. Delay your next contribution until you find out more. You'll decide what to do once you know all the facts.

  b. Send money to another charity. No way are you going to be a sucker.

  c. Continue to give money to the charity. You'd feel guilty about stopping.

SCORING

Find the letter you choose for each number and add up your points.

1. a- 5	b- 1	c- 3
2. a- 1	b- 5	c- 3
3. a- 3	b- 1	c- 5
4. a- 1	b- 3	c- 5
5. a- 3	b- 5	c- 1
6. a- 5	b- 1	c- 3
7. a- 1	b- 3	c- 5
8. a- 5	b- 1	c- 3
9. a- 5	b- 1	c- 3
10. a- 3	b- 5	c- 1
11. a- 1	b- 3	c- 5
12. a- 3	b- 1	c- 5

12 to 28—Minimally Committed
29 to 40—Committed
41 to 60—Overly Committed

✳ Profiles

The points you earned reveal a great deal about your capacity for commitment. Find the profile that describes your functioning in this area.

MINIMALLY COMMITTED

Your answers on the quiz reveal a tendency to switch gears quickly when things in your life don't go the way you planned. While it can be healthy and desirable to make such changes, there is also something to be said for sticking with your original goals and plans. If you give up too readily when you encounter problems, you're likely to find yourself always starting anew instead of following through with what you've already begun.

Chances are that long-term romantic relationships don't come easily to you. You're too impatient to stick around when things aren't to your liking. You'll go to great lengths to protect yourself from becoming vulnerable. When problems occur in a relationship, you're apt to view it as a sign to escape (on a physical or emotional level) before you get hurt.

Looking out for yourself is instinctive with you. Looking out for your relationship is an ability that you probably have not developed. One contributing factor is your lack of faith. Because you're not convinced love can triumph over adversity, you don't see any use in continuing with a troubled relationship. You won't make a sufficient emotional investment to ensure love survives and prospers.

Another factor that reduces your ability to make a commitment is your desire to have everything your own way. If you can't play the game according to your own rules, you don't want to play at all. To negotiate or make concessions seems pointless to you. Love is viewed as worthwhile only when it proceeds exactly as you wish.

The way you deal with change also has implications for your commitment capacity. On the surface, you appear to be very open to change. Instead of suffering through negative occurrences in love or life, you'll take action by ending the relationship or situation. But in reality, you're avoiding change rather than accepting its necessity and inevitability. Your response to change is really a nonresponse.

Unless you're tolerant of the changes that unavoidably occur over time in your partner, your relationship, and yourself, you'll have difficulty making and keeping a commitment to love. Rather than viewing change as an opportunity for growth, you see it as a betrayal of your expectations. You'll want to dissolve the relationship instead of modifying it.

Even if you do remain with your partner for the sake of convenience, your relationship won't be as meaningful and satisfying as it could have been. You won't be together because you believe in what your relationship has been in the past and what it can be in the future.

Commitment is one of the most rewarding aspects of love. There is nothing that can replace the trust, warmth, and devotion of a truly committed relationship. You can learn how to experience this for yourself by reading "Committing Yourself to Love" in the strategies section.

COMMITTED

You're able to make and keep commitments in most areas of your life. You'll readily pledge your support and loyalty to whatever you care about. When you find something or someone you believe in, you're willing to devote the time, energy or money it takes to make it succeed. You try to persevere when you encounter difficulties or obstacles.

Committing yourself to love isn't a problem for you. Maintaining a relationship requires a lot of work, but you have no doubt it's worth it. Once you make an emotional investment, you want to stick with it long enough to reap its reward. Even when things don't go well, you still want to stay with your partner and nurture the relationship so you don't lose all that you've already put into it.

Your ability to try to work out problems can be traced to your trust and faith. You feel that love, like most things in life, is what you make it. You're convinced that a positive attitude and sufficient determination can make love work. Whereas even the slightest suggestion of trouble terrifies some people, you have enough confidence in yourself to know you can handle virtually anything that comes up in the course of your relationship.

But this doesn't mean your sense of commitment has no limits. You'll do everything you possibly can to strengthen and save an ailing relationship, but you're also a realist who recognizes when a relationship has gone beyond the point of no return. When you've exhausted all possibility of salvaging what you once had or had hoped for, you're ready to move on.

You have a healthy resilience that should enable you to deal effectively with the highs and lows of love. You can accept change in your relationship, but you'll also work hard to preserve what has worked in the past. This flexibility leads to an openness to creative compromise and problem-solving. In terms of making and keeping a commitment, you're definitely ready for love.

The strategies section in this chapter is written for people who are less skilled in commitment than you. However, it may be helpful for you to read these pages so you'll know what to do if you should ever find yourself either minimally or excessively committed in the future. Read "Committing Yourself to Love" and "Developing a More Dynamic Commitment to Love" for further insight in how to maximize your commitment ability. Concentrate on "Committing Yourself to Love" if you scored at the low end of the committed range or "Developing a More Dynamic Commitment to Love" if your score was on the upper end. You may even want to read both to gain maximum insight into making the most of your commitment ability.

OVERLY COMMITTED

When you hear about the many people today who have trouble making and keeping a commitment, you really can't identify. You're unable to understand why relationships break up so readily. You're puzzled about why people give up when things become difficult. You simply can't comprehend those individuals who don't share your capacity for commitment in love and life.

While adding up your points on the quiz, you were probably pleased to learn that you fell on the high end of the commitment scale. You may even have felt a little smug. Not only are you loyal, determined, and devoted to the things and people you care about, but you also have more of these qualities than the average person. Surely congratulations are in order for scoring so many points on a quiz about commitment.

Unfortunately, you won't receive any commendations in this book or in your life for being so committed. There's a point where a healthy, desirable capacity for commitment becomes excessive and unhealthy. You appear to have the potential to reach that point. Don't expect any prizes or rewards for being overly committed; you'll only be disappointed at what you end up with.

The problem with your level of commitment is that it negates any possibility for growth in your relationship, your life, or yourself. There is nothing growth-enhancing about sticking with someone or something just because you're too scared to make any changes. This is especially true in love, where you're preventing not only yourself, but also a partner, from developing new and improved ways of loving and being.

Your type of commitment is static. Your main concern is to preserve the status quo at all costs. Maintaining a relationship is more of a priority than enhancing it. You prefer that everything stay exactly the same because that's easier, safer and infinitely more predictable. There's no end to the time or energy you're willing to devote to the impossible quest of making love and life stand still.

The way you deal with change tends to be somewhat of a paradox. On the one hand, you fear and dislike change so much that you'll go to great lengths to prevent it from occurring. One of your favorite strategies may be pretending it doesn't exist. So you may find yourself passively accepting whatever happens in your relationship while denying it's really happening. Instead of effectively dealing with the changes that you, your partner and your life together are bound to experience throughout your relationship, you allow them to occur without monitoring or managing their impact. Resisting and accepting change in this generalized manner is seldom beneficial to love.

You'll be placing yourself at a significant disadvantage in

your love life if you resolutely stick to your original plans and ways of doing things when they no longer work. Continuing a relationship solely because of a commitment you've made in the past is unfair to both you and your partner. Your staying together should be based on an ongoing assessment of your relationship and a determination that it's worth continuing. The strategies section will instruct you in "Developing a More Dynamic Commitment to Love."

✳ Strategies for Improving Your Commitment Capacity

It's not always easy to improve your ability to make and keep a commitment, but it *can* be done. Learn how in this section by reading "Committing Yourself to Love" if you fell on the low end of the commitment scale or "Developing a More Dynamic Commitment to Love" if you're a high scorer.

COMMITTING YOURSELF TO LOVE

Making a commitment to love always involves some risk. There will never be a guarantee of "happily ever after." It would be impossible to eliminate completely the possibility of a relationship not working out in the near or distant future.

But rather than overreact to the potential negatives, you need to focus on the positive aspects of commitment. If you stick with a relationship through good times and bad, and devote sufficient energy to it, you'll be rewarded with true intimacy. You'll have in-depth knowledge of your partner rather than just a superficial awareness of what he or she is all about. You'll be able to communicate with each other with the warmth and ease that develops from your mutual agreement to care about and for each other. You'll also share many experiences and build a history together, which adds meaning to the present and future.

Learning to recognize the value of the status quo can be difficult. You probably lead a fast-paced life that has made you impatient for success and immediate gratification. When your level of accomplishment doesn't conform to your expectations, you see no point in continuing with what has failed to deliver the goods. You'd much rather abandon the here-and-now that isn't quite working to pursue the elusive ideal you might find in the future. But it's essential for you to develop the ability to see why the things you have in the present are worth preserving and improving. This is especially important for your love life, since it can reach its full potential only through your commitment to make it thrive.

Use the worksheet that follows to pinpoint all those reasons why your relationship is worth continuing. If you're not

---

✳   ✳

Check the reason(s) you feel your relationship is worth continuing:

_____ The love we feel or once felt for each other.

_____ The emotional support we give each other.

_____ Compatibility in our life-styles.

_____ Compatibility in our values.

_____ The ability to share our thoughts and feelings with each other.

_____ The time and energy already invested in the relationship.

_____ Companionship.

_____ Good sex.

_____ Safety and security of staying together instead of being on our own or trying different partners.

_____ Raising our children together.

_____ The home we share.

_____ A business we own/run together.

_____ Improved financial status from being together as compared to that we would have separately.

_____ Religious mandates and principles about making and keeping a commitment.

_____ Relatives want us to stay together.

✳   ✳

currently in a relationship, think of a past one and why it might have been worth your while to stick with it.

If you did not check any of the reasons on the worksheet, it's obvious why you would have difficulty with commitment. Without a clear incentive to nurture your relationship, there's no compelling motivation to stick with your partner in rough times. Even if you checked off one or more reasons numbering from seven to fifteen, you will still be lacking any real impetus for staying in the relationship. Safety, security, sex, children, a home, a business, finances, religion, or relatives are not by themselves sufficient reasons to invest in love. Even the desire for companionship is not enough to keep a relationship going. You can always find friends or acquaintances to help ward off loneliness; you're looking for something more in a love relationship. Keep looking until you find it.

If you checked any number from one to six, you need to recognize that you probably have or had a relationship worth preserving. The love you share(d), the emotional investment you've already made, the emotional support, communication, and compatibility are reason enough to do everything you can to make your love work. Once you're aware of the value of your relationship, it should be easier to make and keep a commitment to it.

The next step is to develop faith and trust in love. You need to believe fully that love *can* work, even when you experience some difficult times. Keep your eyes and ears open for examples of couples whose love survived very trying circumstances. If you can begin to see problems and obstacles as challenges rather than indicators for giving up on your relationship, you'll improve your capacity for commitment.

Change and conflict are inevitable in every relationship. Learn to differentiate between what you can handle and what you can't. Instead of automatically viewing new developments in your life together as unacceptable, you need to recognize those you can tolerate and possibly even use to strengthen the relationship. Use the next worksheet to determine the changes and problems you feel you'd be able to deal with in your relationship (either future, current, or past). Since every couple have their own unique circumstances, a few blank spaces are provided to write down any that, although not listed, are relevant to you and your partner.

✳   ✳

Check the changes and problems that you can deal with in your relationship:

_____ Your life together becoming routine or boring.

_____ Your sex life losing its excitement.

_____ Financial problems.

_____ In-law, children, or other family problems.

_____ Leading increasingly separate lives and losing the closeness you had.

_____ Not sharing the same friends.

_____ Not sharing the same interests.

_____ Health problems.

_____ Infidelity.

_____ Your partner becoming more conservative or liberal.

_____ Moving to/living in a different area.

_____ Changes in appearance, including weight.

_____ Changes in your or your partner's status (e.g., career change, success, failure).

_____ Growing older.

_____ Different values and goals.

_____ _____

_____ _____

_____ _____

✳   ✳

For every check you made, look at it as a commitment. You have expressed confidence in your ability to cope with those changes and problems. Should they occur in the course of your relationship, you need to make every effort to work through them. Instead of letting them ruin your relationship, you can try to turn them around and use them as a springboard to develop new and even more effective ways of loving. Even those that appear to be major crises (e.g., financial problems, health concerns, extramarital affairs) can be used to revive and strengthen your love when you face the challenge with courage and compassion. If you should find yourself over-whelmed by your situation, you can seek professional counsel-ing for assistance.

If you've been commitment-phobic for any length of time, you'll experience some discomfort when trying to improve your capacity to stick with a relationship through its ups and downs. It may help if you remember you don't have to go overboard with commitment. Healthy functioning in this area does not mean you have to tolerate anything and everything that occurs in your relationship. There is a point at which it is no longer possible or desirable to continue a relationship. By recognizing what this point is for you, you'll know exactly when it's time to end a commitment. The following worksheet lists a few circumstances under which you may not want to stay in the relationship. Add some of your own as well.

✳   ✳

ESCAPE CLAUSE

Check the circumstance(s) that would cause you to want to end your relationship:

_____ Infidelity.

_____ Substance abuse.

_____ Physical or verbal abuse.

_____ Unresolved family (children, in-laws, other relatives) problems.

_____ Bankruptcy or other severe financial hardship.

_____ Sexual dysfunction.

_____ Incompatibility between your and your partner's religious be-liefs.

_____ Incompatibility between your and your partner's life goals.

_____ Incompatibility between your and your partner's money management (saving and spending styles).

_____ Boredom.

_____ _____

_____ _____

_____ _____

✳   ✳

Now that you've noted the set of circumstances under
which you'd want to break a commitment, those parameters
should make you feel a little more secure. You don't need to
worry about becoming so entrenched in your romantic involvement that you won't know when to escape if irreparable
damage is done. Your escape clause will protect you from
being overly committed.

But making and keeping a commitment may still seem
scary to you, even after completing the previous exercises.
This fear may be lessened by setting smaller and shorter-
term goals for your commitment. Rather than trying to commit to a relationship for the rest of your life, you can break it
down into goals that are less threatening and more immediately attainable.

The two examples on the following worksheet illustrate
achievable goal-setting. Instead of the overambitious goal of
staying together forever no matter what, lesser but still important goals are set for the foreseeable future.

The first example is geared toward someone who is not yet
in a committed relationship. The attainable goal is to date
someone long enough to get to know him rather than just
subjecting the outcome of your acquaintance to your initial
impression and first date. This can be difficult for the type of
person who makes snap judgments. But it only requires a
commitment of six dates, not a lifetime. Making and keeping
this limited commitment has its rewards. A relationship that
might have been abandoned at its very beginning due to
insubstantial reasons is instead given a chance to develop and
blossom. It's a minimal investment for a potential sizable

reward (love). Once the goal of six dates is attained, the next short-term goal could be an exclusive relationship for six months.

The second example depicts a long-term relationship that is currently experiencing stress due to financial difficulty. The goal for commitment is to obtain credit counseling to effectively deal with debt. The reward for attaining this goal is the peace of mind that comes with financial solvency. Once the debt is eliminated or reduced to manageable levels, a new goal could be set of attaining further financial security.

Use the blank worksheet to record your own short-term commitment goal, rewards for goal attainment, and the next goal you'll work on after you attain the first. It will require some hard work and determination to keep this commitment, but you'll reap many benefits from doing so. By improving your capacity to make and keep a commitment, you'll be much more ready for love.

❊   ❊

COMMITMENT GOAL: Go out with someone long enough (e.g., six dates) to really get to know him before making any decisions about whether the relationship could work over the long-term.

REWARDS FOR ATTAINING THIS GOAL: By giving a new relationship a chance, I may discover that it's more promising than it originally appeared.

THE NEXT GOAL: Date him exclusively for six months.

❊   ❊

❊   ❊

COMMITMENT GOAL: To make sure that money problems don't ruin our relationship, obtain credit counseling so we can handle all our debts better.

REWARDS FOR ATTAINING THIS GOAL: Increased financial and psychological security; less fighting about our money problems.

THE NEXT GOAL: Adhering to a workable budget that includes putting aside some money for savings, emergencies, and special purchases.

❊   ❊

```
*                                                              *

  COMMITMENT GOAL: _____

  _____

  REWARDS FOR ATTAINING THIS GOAL: _____

  _____

  _____

  THE NEXT GOAL: _____

  _____

  _____

*                                                              *
```

DEVELOPING A MORE DYNAMIC COMMITMENT TO LOVE

Scoring as high as you did on the quiz, you certainly don't need to learn how to increase your capacity for commitment. You're a highly committed person who has no difficulty in remaining loyal and faithful to whatever you care about. In the area of love, you can easily make and keep a lifelong commitment, honoring it at all costs and under any circumstances.

But you do have room for improvement in the way you commit yourself to love. Because your major concern is to preserve the status quo no matter what, you're likely to try to make love stand still. By passively ignoring or actively resisting new developments that occur in your relationship and life, you prevent any opportunity for growth. You maintain a static commitment to love, and this can cause your relationship to become stagnant.

With a little effort, you can develop a more dynamic commitment to love. Instead of doing all you can to guard against any changes in your relationship, you should learn to discern between those that have positive implications and those that have a negative impact. If, for example, your partner develops an interest in a hobby or sport that you don't share, this doesn't necessarily spell doom for your relationship. Rather than resent his or her absorption in this new activity and discourage its pursuit, you can learn to recognize its value to both of you. Not only will your partner have an increased sense of satisfaction and well-being that will spread to other areas, such as your relationship, chances are you'll get along better and have more to talk about.

Even traumatic events can eventually result in something positive. Illness and financial failure often force their victims to take stock of their lives and reassess their priorities. By discovering what's really important, former life-styles can be completely turned around, and more satisfying ways of life may develop in their place.

Use the following worksheet to pinpoint which potential changes you find most threatening. If you're not currently in a relationship, base your choices on a past relationship (using either those changes you worried about or ones that actually did interfere with your ability and desire to stay together).

---

*   *

Choose the three items that cause you the greatest fear, anxiety, or discomfort in terms of their impact upon your past or current relationship:

_____ Illness or injury (that falls upon you).

_____ Illness or injury (that falls upon your partner).

_____ Substance abuse (yours or your partner's).

_____ Problems with your children.

_____ Problems with either set of parents or other relatives.

_____ Job loss (yours).

_____ Job loss (your partner's).

_____ Problems with your job.

_____ Problems with your partner's job.

_____ A job transfer and consequent move.

_____ Interference from or trouble with friends.

_____ Financial debt/bankruptcy.

_____ Not having enough money for luxuries.

_____ Not having enough money to keep up your current standard of living.

_____ Not attaining your dreams.

_____ Your partner not attaining his or her dreams.

_____ Your growing older.

_____ Your partner growing older.

_____ Infidelity.

_____ Boredom.

_____ Declining sex life.

_____ Developing separate interests.

_____ Developing separate values.

_____ _____

_____ _____

_____ _____

✳   ✳

Now that you've selected three items, the next exercise will help you sort out your feelings about the potential change or occurrence. It will also assist you in delineating the reality of the situation by forcing you to recognize the potential positive implications. This is followed by a strategy to maximize the positive impact.

The example illustrates the potential change or occurrence of a job transfer and consequent move. If you dread the thought of moving away and leaving behind familiar people and places, you might tend to focus on the negatives of the move. The potential move could cause a great deal of friction between you and your partner since he or she may resent your reluctance to move despite a wonderful job opportunity. But by taking a few minutes to reflect on the situation, you might come up with some positive implications, such as improved finances or the excitement of exploring a new city. In the strategies section, some plans for actions to enhance the positive impact are outlined.

✳   ✳

POTENTIAL CHANGE OR OCCURRENCE: A job transfer and consequent move.

YOUR CONCERNS ABOUT IT: We'd be leaving behind an area we know and love, as well as a supportive network of family and friends. I would have to look for a new job.

POTENTIAL POSITIVE IMPLICATIONS OF THE CHANGE OR OCCUR-RENCE: Sharing the adventure of discovering new places and making new friends, which could add some excitement to our relationship; lower cost of living combined with a big salary increase, which would help alleviate much of our financial stress; possibility of having a job that is better than the one I now have.

STRATEGIES FOR ENHANCING THE POSITIVE IMPACT: Try to maintain an open mind about the transfer. Research the new area to make an informed decision about whether to move and to be able to quickly settle in the new area if the move does occur.

✳   ✳

Use the blank worksheet to map out one of the changes or occurrences you selected in the previous worksheet. When you take a few minutes to outline the implications and ways of maximizing the positive aspects, you'll see that most new developments in your life and love don't have to be feared. Instead of working against change, you can make it work for you in keeping your relationship fresh and challenging.

✳   ✳

POTENTIAL CHANGE OR OCCURRENCE: _____

_____

YOUR CONCERNS ABOUT IT: _____

_____

_____

POTENTIAL POSITIVE IMPLICATIONS OF THE CHANGE OR
OCCURRENCE:

_____

_____

STRATEGIES FOR ENHANCING THE POSITIVE IMPACT:

_____

_____

_____

✳   ✳

Of course, it would be absurd to suggest that you have to
embrace every change or event that occurs. There will be
things you can't handle, nor should you have to. You need to
mentally set some points of no return so that you'll know when
it's time to end a commitment. The next worksheet will help
you pinpoint those conditions that would lead you to terminate
a relationship. Use the blank lines to write in some additional
circumstances under which you should or would not want to
continue your commitment. Once you acknowledge what you
find unacceptable in a relationship, you'll be better able to
work at ensuring that yours doesn't get to that point. You'll
still be committed to love, but in a much more dynamic way.

✳   ✳

POINT OF NO RETURN

Check the circumstance(s) that would cause you to want to end your relationship:

_____ Infidelity.

_____ Substance abuse.

_____ Physical or verbal abuse.

_____ Unresolved family (children, in-laws, other relatives) problems.

_____ Bankruptcy or other severe financial hardship.

_____ Sexual dysfunction.

_____ Incompatibility between your and your partner's religious beliefs.

_____ Incompatibility between your and your partner's life goals.

_____ Incompatibility between your and your partner's money management (spending and saving styles).

_____ Boredom.

_____ _____

_____ _____

_____ _____

✳   ✳

RECOMMENDED READING

Jeffers, Susan. *Opening Our Hearts to Men*. New York: Fawcett Columbine, 1989.

O'Neill, Nena, and George O'Neill. *Open Marriage*. New York: Evans, 1972 and 1984.

Sternberg, Robert J. *The Triangle of Love*. New York: Basic Books, 1988.

Is There Room in Your Life for Love?

When you love someone, that person becomes an important part of your life. If you're currently involved in a relationship, you're already sharing your life to some degree. If you're eagerly looking for love, you probably feel there's something missing in your life and would gladly make room in it to accommodate someone special.

Most people can find at least a little room in their lives to include the person they love most. But for many of us, it can be difficult to find the ideal balance between living such a full life that there's not enough room for someone else and having a life that is so empty that it promotes extreme neediness and dependency.

The space in your life that you've allotted for love has significant implications for your success in loving and being loved. This concept of room in your life for love goes beyond the physical commodities of time and energy. It encompasses something far less tangible: the *need* and the *opportunities* you have for letting someone into your life.

Take the following quiz to determine how much room is available in your life, then read the corresponding profiles. The strategies section at the end offers suggestions on what to do if your life has too much or too little room for love.

✳   **Q U I Z**   ✳

There are many things that can fill up a life. Read the descriptions of the various people, activities, and responsibilities and then rate them according to their importance in your personal world. Your life may not contain everything listed, but take a few minutes to consider which ones play crucial roles.

Activities

CAREER
   Full-time and/or part-time job(s).
      Includes actual work time and demands, as well as other related activities (e.g., commuting, reading professional and business publications, attending seminars and workshops and networking after regular work hours).
      If you're a full-time student, you can consider attending classes and studying to be your work.

ACTIVE LEISURE
   Activities on an avocational basis pursued for fun rather than for monetary gain or health purposes.
      Includes hobbies (such as arts and crafts, creative writing, gardening), clubs and organizations, games (e.g., bridge or backgammon) and physical activities where pleasure is the goal rather than fitness (such as bowling, splashing around in a pool, hang-gliding).
      Does not include activities purely for relaxation (such as watching television or listening to music) or socializing purposes (e.g., visiting with friends).

PASSIVE LEISURE
   Activities pursued on a solitary basis for rest and relaxation, with minimal energy demands.
      Includes television, movies/video, music, reading for fun rather than for intellectual stimulation or business/educational requirements, naps, nonreligious meditation, playing with pets.
      Does not include more active leisure pursuits or social activities with friends.

TRAVEL
Activities that remove you from your home and place you in a different environment, undertaken on a voluntary basis rather than for business purposes or for family obligations.
Includes trips of at least sixty miles or more and for a day or longer duration (e.g., weekend or week-long trips) to any destination (rural or urban).

INTELLECTUAL PURSUITS
Activities pursued for intellectual stimulation.
Includes classes that are undertaken for personal growth rather than for a degree, reading for information (e.g., newspapers, magazines, nonfiction books), news on TV or radio, as well as cultural events that expand horizons (such as attending performances of unfamiliar or challenging music, plays, dance).
Does not include work-related or continuing education courses.

SPIRITUALITY
Activities of a religious or spiritual nature.
Includes worship services, church activities, individual prayer, meditation and study.

VOLUNTEER/CIVIC WORK
Activities performed without pay for the betterment of your community or the world at large.
Includes all nonreimbursed work for human service, environmental, political and other organizations.

SHOPPING
Activities related to the ultimate acquisition of goods and services.
Includes reading catalogs and ads, browsing in stores and shopping for specific items.

PERSONAL UPKEEP
Activities to maintain your appearance and health.
Includes eating, sleeping, grooming, food preparation, personal laundry and medical care.
Does not include physical fitness activities.

PHYSICAL FITNESS
Activities to keep your body in shape.
Includes active sports and exercise, with the goal(s) of improving endurance, strength, tone, cardiovascular functioning.
Does not include physical activities done just for fun (such as slow dancing or walking).

HOUSEHOLD UPKEEP
Activities to keep your home (house, condo, apartment) in order.
Includes cleaning, household laundry, decorating, pet care, plant care, budgeting/money management and investing.

CHILDREN
Activities with or for your children.
Includes chauffeuring to lessons and appointments, playing with children, parent-teacher conferences and making plans for your child's future.

RELATIVES
Activities with or for your family.
Includes parents, siblings and other relatives.
Does not include own children.

FRIENDS
Activities with or for your friends.
Includes visiting in person and on the phone.

IMPORTANCE IN YOUR LIFE

0—Not part of your life at all.
1—Minimal importance in your life.
2—Moderate importance in your life.
3—Substantial importance in your life.
4—Absorbs a major part of your life.

Now rate the following activities/people/responsibilities in terms of their current importance in your life by putting a check in the appropriate box.

SCORING

Once you've obtained totals for each of the four columns (note that the zero column always totals zero, no matter how many items you've checked), you can add the four numbers together to obtain your final score. This score can range from 0 to 56. Chances are you fall somewhere in between these two extremes.

0 to 21—Excessive room in your life for love.
22 to 32—Adequate room in your life for love.
33 to 56—Minimal room in your life for love.

Find the profile that best describes the room in your life and learn more about how it affects your ability to love and be loved.

	0	1	2	3	4
Career					
Active Leisure					
Passive Leisure					
Travel					
Intellectual Pursuits					
Spirituality					
Volunteer/Civic Work					
Shopping					
Personal Upkeep					
Physical Fitness					
Household Upkeep					
Children					
Relatives					
Friends					
TOTAL of each column (count the number of checks in each column and multiply by the number on top)	0				

✳ Profiles

Find the profile that corresponds with your quiz results.

EXCESSIVE ROOM IN YOUR LIFE FOR LOVE

There are both positive and negative aspects to all the room that's currently available in your life. First, the good news: Because you have so much unfilled space in your world, there's plenty of room for someone else. You won't have to scramble to find time or energy for love; you should have more than enough of both.

Nor is there any question about the need for something more in your life. Almost everyone will profess a need for love, but a significant number of individuals never reserve a place for it in their lives. You probably feel more of a desire for a loving relationship than do other people whose lives are fuller. You know that your life is far from complete and have no doubt your life would be empty without someone you love who loves you back.

Because love is so important to you, you'll do whatever it takes to find and keep it. If you're currently looking for love, you'll devote a great deal of effort to the quest. You'll focus a majority of your thoughts on the type of person you want and how to meet that special someone. Once you're involved in a relationship, you continue to give it your full attention. You probably won't be content just to let it coast while you both live your lives; instead, you'll dedicate yourself to the relationship, allowing it to assume utmost importance while everything else in your life pales by comparison.

With the incredibly busy lives most of us lead these days, it's easy for couples to lose touch with each other and never really connect in a meaningful way. But that's highly unlikely to occur in *your* relationship. Rather than living a life that is separate and distinct from your partner's, for you togetherness is the rule rather than the exception. Unlike other people who feel that their respective partners are neglecting them, your spouse or significant other knows that he or she takes priority over everything else in your life. You'll see to it that you spend lots of time with each other and share all you can.

There's no question you have an ample amount of room in your life for love. You need love and you have many opportunities to accommodate it within your life. You're definitely ready for love in this regard.

But now the bad news: It's neither fair nor realistic to expect love to fill all the gaps in your life. Love can add a lot to your life, but it can't do it all. You need to have a life of your own before you can share it with someone else. Scoring as low as you did on the scale reveals the unfortunate fact that you haven't developed a life that is rewarding in its own right. Instead, you rely much too heavily on your partner and your relationship to make a satisfactory life.

On the surface, there may not appear to be anything wrong with this reliance on love to make your life complete. After all, love definitely fulfills a need for most people and provides the missing piece to the jigsaw puzzle of life. But there are too many pieces missing from *your* life. The emptiness is too extreme to be filled completely by love. No matter how hard you try, you'll never be able to achieve wholeness and happiness solely through love. Attempting to use love to this end will cause problems for both you and your partner.

One negative consequence is the tendency to become unhappy with your partner when you continue to experience an emptiness in your life. If you've convinced yourself love is *the* answer to the boredom or the lack of fulfillment that plagues you, it's inevitable that you'll be extremely disappointed when you discover these problems still exist even once you find love. Your partner may be an interesting and giving person, but he or she has his or her own life to live and can't totally make one for you. You can easily become disenchanted and even resentful when love doesn't magically erase all your needs and problems.

Another major concern is the neediness and dependency that an empty life can provoke. When you don't have much going on in your life, there's an increased likelihood of latching on to someone else's life with the hope of filling in the missing pieces. Adapting to another person's life-style is one thing, but you're apt to go overboard and attempt to live his or her life completely. This can be flattering at first to a partner, but it soon becomes cloying and suffocating. Your partner needs some space and time away from you, but you may not allow him or her to have it. You feel hurt when he or she doesn't want to share all aspects of his or her life with you, and may react with tears, tantrums, accusations and ultimatums. Your partner may respond in turn with guilt, anger or apathy. A vicious cycle may develop as he or she tries to establish some distance from you when you become too clinging, which causes you to become even more needy or demanding, which then results in your partner's withdrawing even more.

Another disadvantage to your lacking a sufficient life of your own is that you don't contribute enough to the relationship. You take from your partner without giving anything back. Your partner will be deprived of the stimulation that someone else's interests, friends and activities can bring to his or her life. Instead of you both living your own lives *and* sharing a life together, the two of you will be living practically the same life. Unless your partner wants a clone (and few people do), he or she may be forced eventually to seek the companionship of someone more capable of both complementing and contrasting with his or her perspectives and experiences.

But things don't have to remain this way. With a little effort on your part, you can expand the scope and focus of your life beyond your need for love. Your partner can still be a priority in your life, but you can learn to cultivate and enjoy other relationships and experiences. Read the strategies section on "Saving Room for Love While Making a Life for Yourself" for further details.

ADEQUATE ROOM IN YOUR LIFE FOR LOVE

You've achieved a balanced life-style that combines sufficient room for love with a full roster of your own interests, activities and friends. Love is important to you and you've saved enough space in your life to accommodate it, but not at the expense of all the other things that life can offer. While you want to share part of your life with someone special, you also want to pursue some of it on your own.

Unlike those who have too much or too little room in their lives for love, you're able to be part of a "we" while still retaining the "me." Your identity and independence can be preserved, allowing you to live life in the way that is most meaningful to you. This enables you to be a happy, fulfilled and interesting mate for your partner. At the same time, your life isn't so full that you lack the time or energy for love. For a complete life, you need to include a loving relationship. This desire for love will compel you to do everything possible to find it and make it last.

If you haven't yet found love, you'll want to continue looking for it. By continuing your life the way you're currently living it, you stand a good chance of meeting Mr. or Ms. Right. You may want to add a few more activities and expand your social network to enhance the odds of connecting with that special person. Once you do meet a promising individual, you can immediately include him or her in your life.

If you're already in a loving relationship, you're probably sharing a great deal together while still pursuing your own individual lives. Your life may be busy and even hectic at times, but you should still be able to find enough space in it to nurture love.

Your score may have been on the low end (i.e., 22 to 24) of the "adequate room" spectrum. If so, you may want to read the strategies section on "Saving Room for Love While Making a Life for Yourself" to learn how to make your life a little fuller and thus reduce the potential for neediness and dependency. If your score was on the higher end of the "adequate room" spectrum (i.e., 30 to 32), it may be helpful for you to read the strategies section addressing "Making Room for Love" to ensure that you never let your life get too full for love.

MINIMAL ROOM IN YOUR LIFE FOR LOVE

You lead the type of life that less busy people may envy. To a person who's a little bored with his or her own life, yours seems to have everything that his or hers lacks. Unlike other people, you never have the problem of not enough to do. There's so much filling your life that you probably find yourself wishing that you had more time or energy to make the most of it all.

You're obviously in no danger of becoming a clinging, dependent person who latches on to a partner. To the contrary, you'll lead your own life with a minimum of demands or expectations for your loved one. It's highly unlikely your partner will ever feel suffocated by too much togetherness. He or she will be free to pursue personal interests without being dragged down by a mate who needs maximum assistance in making a fulfilling life.

Similarly, there's virtually no chance of your partner ever finding you boring. You bring constant stimulation into your partner's life through the full roster of people and activities you cultivate. Even though your mate may not be actively involved with all these things or people, he or she is exposed to them through your participation and vicariously experiences them. Just listening to your conversation about your world helps expand his or her own.

Another benefit of your full life is that it provides you with an extensive support system. Whereas some couples are socially isolated and have only each other, your involvement in so many activities and interaction with large numbers of people ensures that you'll have plenty of friends and acquaintances. These people can offer advice, encouragement, and reassurance when you need it, in addition to filling in the gaps of your relationship and providing what your partner (as just one person) cannot. Whenever you encounter some problems in your life, this support system can take some of the heat off your partner so you do not depend exclusively on him or her to help you work it all out.

But the negative consequences of minimal room in your life for love far outweigh the advantages. Although self-reliance is an admirable quality, when carried to an extreme it denies your partner the opportunity to feel needed. If he or she doesn't feel like an integral part of your life, your partner may be unhappy being relegated to such a limited role. Whereas he or she wants a leading role in your life, you've cast your loved one into an inconsequential minor part, which could easily be disposed of without significantly impacting the rest of your life. The only way your partner may be willing to accept this is if he or she leads a similarly overloaded life that doesn't have time for *you*! Otherwise, most people would want more time and attention than you're currently able to give.

With time and energy being finite resources, you lack enough of each to find love or make it work. You've chosen instead to use the resources for everything but your partner. You probably devote more attention to your relationships with friends, family and coworkers than to the person you claim to love most. When love is neglected rather than nourished, your relationship will remain stagnant at best and can even deteriorate to the point where you lose all emotional intimacy and function as strangers rather than lovers.

On the rare occasions where you and your partner do manage to connect, you may be shocked to discover you've been growing at different rates and in different directions as you pursued your separate lives. There is never any guarantee that a couple will experience similar personal growth over the course of their relationship. But because you haven't left enough room in your life to share some of it with your partner, the odds of developing divergent goals and interests are increased. Without a concerted effort to stay connected, you can easily become two people with little in common and no real reason to stay together.

The need for sufficient room in your life for love holds true whether you've been with your partner for two months or twenty years. Both new and long-standing relationships must be treated as a priority in your life. You may have lots of other things and people in it, but love has to come first. An occasional halfhearted effort at togetherness may appease some guilt about not putting more time and energy into the relationship, but it won't be enough to make and seal a real bond between the two of you.

It's also essential to have adequate room in your life when you're in the process of searching for love. You may feel that you want someone to love and be loved by, but the way you live your life may preclude this desire from ever becoming a reality. If you've created a high comfort level for yourself with the schedule, activities and people of your choosing, it could be more difficult than you realize to let someone else into your life. Some modification of your current life is inevitable once you begin to share it with the person you love, so it's best to have a little space available from the outset to facilitate rearranging your priorities and commitments.

"Having it all" is an appealing concept, but it's close to impossible to advance it beyond the fantasy stage. If you want to be successful in love, you need to make room for it in your life by giving up other things that may not be quite as fulfilling or as important as love. You may not be able to have it all, but you can have the best of what life can offer: love. The strategies section will assist you in doing this by "Making Room for Love."

❋ Strategies for Having the Right Amount of Room in Your Life for Love

There's no getting around the need for an optimal amount of room in your life for love. If the quiz revealed you have excessive room, read the section on "Saving Room for Love While Making a Life for Yourself." If your score placed you in the minimal room category, you need to turn to the section on "Making Room for Love."

SAVING ROOM FOR LOVE WHILE MAKING A LIFE FOR YOURSELF

The surplus of available space in your life may reflect a deliberate effort on your part to reserve your time and energy for love. You may feel nothing is more important than love and consequently have devoted a major part of your life to looking for love or to ensuring that your relationship gets the attention it deserves.

But it's equally possible that the overabundance of room in your life represents a lack of action or thought on your part, the available space developing and increasing on its own because you've neglected to make a fuller life for yourself. Fear, apathy, or lack of knowledge about all the options available may have prevented you from creating a satisfying life. Although you may not be able to articulate exactly what is missing from your life, you probably sense an emptiness and may experience some yearning to fill that void. When you see other people enjoying full lives that include love, you may convince yourself love is the key ingredient and your world would automatically expand if you got more love into it (by either enhancing your current relationship or beginning a new one). While waiting for this to happen, you continue to live in limbo, delaying taking any steps to improve your life.

You're correct in many of your assumptions and expectations about love. It's true a love relationship broadens both partners' horizons. It's also true you need to allot sufficient room in your life for love. Whether you're looking for love or already have it, your life should have enough space in it for you to need love and for you to have adequate opportunities to let someone else into your life. But you err in going overboard in leaving so much emptiness in your life. A certain amount of room is beneficial, but too much is undesirable. You won't have enough to offer your partner and will be much too dependent on him or her if you don't have a life of your own.

The solution is obvious enough. You must make a meaningful and fulfilling life for yourself, while being careful to save room for love. You need to fill your life with enough activities, people and responsibilities to enable you to be your own person; at the same time, you can't get so engrossed in all the other parts of your life that you no longer need to share some of it with a partner. The way to achieve this balance is to take actions that will increase the score you obtained in the quiz to the 22 to 32 range. If your score is less than 22, you'll still be in the position of having a life with too much room for love. If you go to extremes and obtain a score significantly over 32 points, you'll have succeeded too well in fulfilling your life and will then be faced with trying to make enough room for love!

Determining which aspects of your life to become more involved in isn't easy. Reaching that optimal score of 22 to 32 on terms most comfortable for you will require a positive attitude toward change and a willingness to experiment and possibly fail. Only through trial and error will you ultimately arrive at your goal of having the right amount of room in your life for love.

Use the worksheet that follows to select three areas you'd like to make more important in your life. Look at the original chart you filled in at the beginning of this chapter and find some areas you originally rated low (0 to 1) but are now

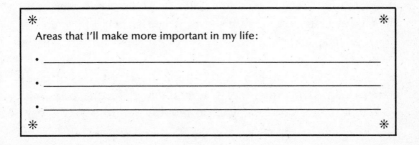

✻   ✻
  Areas that I'll make more important in my life:

  • _____

  • _____

  • _____
✻   ✻

striving to increase to 3 or 4. Any combination of categories is okay. For example, you might focus on career, physical fitness, and spirituality, or friends, travel, and leisure as just two possible combinations.

Now that you know where you're headed, the next issue is *how* to get there. . . . You need to plan some realistic strategies for making a fuller life for yourself, especially in the three priority areas you just pinpointed. If, for example, you've selected your career as a targeted area, you can obtain professional career counseling, attend continuing education seminars or undertake a new project to make your work life more satisfying. Enhancing the active leisure part of your life is as easy as pursuing any activity that interests you, be it jewelry making or rock climbing. For passive leisure, you can experiment with different techniques to promote mental health and physical relaxation (i.e., biofeedback or meditation). Travel, intellectual pursuits and spirituality can be expanded to play a bigger role in your life. You can map out strategies for taking better care of yourself in the personal upkeep and physical fitness areas. Household upkeep can be enhanced by putting more effort into keeping your home clean or decorating it in a way that gives you maximum pleasure.

As for the people in your life, you need to be sure that children (if you have them) are treated as a priority by giving them quality time in shared activities. To establish more closeness with relatives, decide what you need to do to fully connect with your family (such as regular phone calls, frequent visits, better communication). If you want more and closer relationships, establish your own rituals and increase your efforts to bring more people into your life and foster intimacy.

Use the next worksheet to establish some personal goals and plans. After you read the examples, fill out your own sheet for one of the areas you targeted.

✳   ✳

TARGETED AREA: Career

GOAL: Find an alternative type of work that I'd enjoy more.

PLANS FOR ACHIEVING THE GOAL:
1. Speak with friends and acquaintances about their work and ask for their suggestions on career possibilities.
2. Try some part-time jobs or volunteer work in different areas to see whether I'd like that type of work.
3. Consult a career counselor or reputable employment agency.

✳   ✳

✳   ✳

TARGETED AREA: Friends

GOAL: Establish three new friendships in the next six months.

PLANS FOR ACHIEVING THE GOAL:
1. Join a social organization.
2. Ask a new coworker out to lunch.
3. Invite a neighbor I hardly know over for coffee.
4. Accept the next invitation I get to a party, wedding or other social function.

✳   ✳

✳   ✳

TARGETED AREA: _____

GOAL: _____

_____

PLANS FOR ACHIEVING THE GOAL:

_____

_____

_____

_____

_____

✳   ✳

Once you make your life a little fuller, you'll reduce your potential for neediness and dependency. You'll be more interesting to a partner, as well as to yourself. Love will then be able to play an important part in your life, but not in an unhealthy or all-consuming way. You'll truly be able to make the most of love, whether you're trying to find love or improve a relationship.

MAKING ROOM IN YOUR LIFE FOR LOVE

Take a few deep breaths before reading on. What you'll be asked to do here will be difficult and even painful at times. There won't be any surprises; you already know what needs to be done. Your life needs to be streamlined so you can find more room for love. And you need to start doing this right now. If you postpone it until tomorrow, you'll go another day without being able to share your life fully with the person you care about. Love is obviously something you're interested in maximizing, or you wouldn't be reading this book. So don't deny yourself the opportunity to improve your love ability.

If only there were more than twenty-four hours in a day . . . if only human beings had unlimited energy . . . if only you could continue to pursue your extremely busy life as it is now *and* have enough room for love, too. . . .

But there's no way to turn these musings and wishes into reality. You've got to work with what you have, and what you have are finite resources of time and energy. To really need love and have opportunities to enjoy it in your life, you'll need to give up some of the people and activities that currently demand so much of your attention.

It would be impossible to terminate abruptly all your present relationships, interests and commitments. There are people who count on you (friends, family, coworkers, bosses, organizations) to be there for them. While they may gradually learn to decrease their dependency on you, they need time and preparation to do so. There are also responsibilities that you're now obligated to fulfill and that can't be stopped until you make other arrangements. Whether it's a houseful of plants or an ongoing weekly commitment for volunteer work, you can't suddenly rid yourself of these responsibilities just because you've made a decision to free up your life. You have to give notice or find someone else to perform these duties before you're really off the hook.

Nor would it be emotionally healthy for you to stop doing all those things that have given pleasure and meaning to your life. You'll have to delete some aspects of your current life, but certainly not everything. If you clear out your life so there's almost nothing left, you'll then be faced with an emptiness that can promote apathy, anxiety and depression. Having too much room in your life will make you a less desirable love partner because you'll cling to and possibly even suffocate your loved one by attempting to live his or her life to compensate for the lack of your own.

The total score you received in the quiz revealed that many activities and people are important to you. The idea now is not to reduce your score to the point where there's almost nothing of importance remaining (i.e., 17 or below). What you need to do is reduce your score to 36 points or below. Ideally, you should aim for the 22 to 32 range.

Getting to this point will necessitate decreasing some of your original ratings in the first worksheet of this chapter from 3 and 4 to 0, 1 or 2. The lowered rating represents diminished importance and involvement in your life, so give some thought as to what will be easiest for you to give up and what you'd most like to hang onto at your current level of involvement. To begin the process of making more room in your life, choose three areas from the original chart as the ones you've targeted to become less involved in.

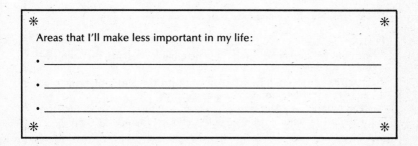

✳   ✳
Areas that I'll make less important in my life:

• _____

• _____

• _____
✳   ✳

Your next step is to develop concrete strategies for lessening your involvement in the areas you delineated. Just lowering your numerical rating isn't sufficient; you must develop some attainable goals and realistic plans for becoming less involved in the targeted areas. You may, for example, want to consider slightly lowering the importance of your career in your life and, consequently, the time and energy it takes away from other things, such as love. If you're very involved in recreational activities, you may decide to pare your list of leisure pastimes to the ones that bring you the most pleasure. Travel, intellectual pursuits, volunteer/civic work, shopping, personal/household upkeep and physical fitness can also be trimmed to make more room in your life for love.

The demands people make on your time and energy can be a little more difficult to cut back on. But it's important you learn to accept that you can't be all things to all people. You can't neglect your children, but it's self-defeating to try to be a superparent. You must learn to be satisfied with what you can realistically do. If your family places unreasonable demands on you or has expectations that you can't live up to, you'll need to learn to say no without feeling guilty. With friends who may want more from you than you're able to give, you can't allow them to become overly needy or clinging.

The next worksheet requires you to finalize your goals and plans for one of the targeted areas you want to decrease your involvement in. A couple of examples are offered to start you off, but then you're on your own.

✳   ✳

TARGETED AREA: Volunteer/civic work.

GOAL: Limit my involvement to four hours a week.

PLANS FOR ACHIEVING THE GOAL:
1. Give the Volunteer Director at the hospital my resignation (with two weeks' notice).
2. Explore the possibilities of doing work for the Sierra Club instead, since the environment is my major concern.
3. Read a book on assertiveness to learn how to say no gracefully the next time a parent in my child's class asks me to undertake a project.

✳   ✳

❋   ❋

TARGETED AREA: Physical fitness.

GOAL: Maintain my current weight, tone, and stamina with only three exercise sessions a week.

PLANS FOR ACHIEVING THE GOAL:
1. Consult a personal fitness/athletic trainer for suggestions on the type of exercise that's best for me.
2. Try jump-roping to see if I like it (since one of my friends claims she gets a terrific aerobic workout from it).
3. Commit myself to three days every week when I'll exercise, by writing it in my appointment book or calendar, and only exercise on these days.

❋   ❋

❋   ❋

TARGETED AREA: _____

GOAL: _____

_____

PLANS FOR ACHIEVING THIS GOAL:

_____

_____

_____

_____

❋   ❋

You may fear that streamlining your life in the ways suggested in this section will result in an emptiness that you find uncomfortable and unfulfilling. This couldn't be further from the truth. The whole purpose of creating more room in your life is to make sure you can accommodate love in it. You'll be giving some things up, but you'll also be gaining something very important—an increased ability to love and be loved.

RECOMMENDED READING

Beck, Aaron T. *Love Is Never Enough*. San Francisco: Harper & Row, 1988.

Dowling, Colette. *The Cinderella Complex: Women's Hidden Fear of Independence*. New York: Pocket Books, 1978.

Eichenbaum, Luise, and Susie Orbach. *What Do Women Want? Exploding the Myth of Female Dependency*. New York: Coward, McCann, and Geoghegan, 1983.

Emery, Gary. *Own Your Own Life*. New York: New American Library, 1982.

Freeman, Arthur, and Rose De Wolf. *Woulda/Shoulda/Coulda*. New York: Morrow, 1989.

Katz, Stan J., and Aimee E. Liu. *False Love and Other Romantic Illusions*. New York: Ticknor & Felds, 1988.

Price, Stephen, and Susan Price. *No More Lonely Nights*. New York: Putnam, 1988.

Schaeffer, Brenda. *Is It Love or Is It Addiction?* New York: Harper/Hazelden, 1987.

Wegscheider-Cruise, Sharon. *Coupleship*. Deerfield Beach, Florida: Health Communications, 1988.

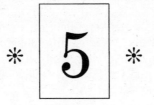

Can You Use Money to Support and Enhance Love?

Although the Beatles noted in song that love couldn't be bought, in real life they probably wouldn't have denied that money does have a significant impact on a relationship. No amount of money can buy real love, but love can be adversely affected by the way money is regarded and handled by both partners.

Each of us comes to a relationship with certain perspectives about money. As children, we developed attitudes, beliefs, fears, and hopes regarding financial matters, which aren't easily abandoned as we reach adulthood. Our experiences as grownups may somewhat modify our money philosophy and approach, but we continue to have our unique money styles. When our style clashes with our partner's, serious conflicts can result.

It's easy enough to say glibly that money and love should be entirely separate and one shouldn't affect the other. In actuality, they're irrevocably interconnected. For better or worse, money is a part of our lives. How we handle it has everything to do with who we are. So once we enter into a love relationship, money becomes part of the package.

Ideally, money should be used to support love on a day-to-day and long-term basis. While it shouldn't be the end-all in a relationship, it can and should be a means for couples to enjoy security for the future while having pleasure in the present. If you have difficulty achieving this balance, it could have a negative impact upon your ability to love and be loved.

Your own money style will be indicated in the quiz that follows and then described in terms of how it affects love. The strategies section offers some suggestions for using money to enhance (not interfere with) love.

✳   **Q U I Z**   ✳

Choose the most appropriate answer.

1. The job you would most likely accept:
   a. Has good potential for advancement.
   b. Pays the highest salary possible.
   c. Offers financial security (e.g., stability and a great pension plan).

2. Which motto best expresses your personal money philosophy?
   a. The person who dies with the most toys wins.
   b. A penny saved is a penny earned.
   c. Money can't buy happiness, but it *can* buy some pretty terrific things.

3. The book you'd be most likely to read is:
   a. *How to Save Money and Accumulate a Million Dollars.*
   b. *How to Use Money Wisely.*
   c. *How to Live Like a Millionaire.*

4. While shopping, you fall in love with a sweater that costs much more than you usually spend on clothes. What do you do?
   a. Treat yourself because you deserve it.
   b. Forget it; there's no way you'd consider spending that kind of money.
   c. Think for a while about whether you could afford it and try to work it into your budget.

5. Which of the following is most difficult for you?
  a. Saving money.
  b. Devoting enough time to thinking about and dealing with financial matters.
  c. Spending money without feeling guilty.

6. If a relative died and left you $50,000, you would:
  a. Spend part of in on something you've always dreamed about (e.g., a vacation or starting your own business) and invest the rest.
  b. Save it all.
  c. Use it to buy all those things you wanted but couldn't afford before.

7. If your salary was cut by 20 percent, it would really hurt because you:
  a. Couldn't save as much money as you'd like.
  b. Would have to make some changes in the present life-style you enjoy.
  c. Would have to get a part-time job to make up the difference so you could continue your spending habits.

8. Your approach to Christmas gift-giving is to:
  a. Throw caution to the wind and buy whatever seems right, regardless of the cost; after all, it's Christmas!
  b. Decide on the exact amount you want to spend on each present and then purchase something in that price range.
  c. Find gifts you know the recipients will like and buy them if they fit your budget.

9. In a restaurant, when studying the menu, you:
  a. Order whatever you want with little or no regard for the price.
  b. Look at the prices first and choose the cheaper items.
  c. Read the entire menu and order what you like if the price isn't too exorbitant.

10. Have you ever had a problem where you overextended yourself with credit?
  a. Never.
  b. Frequently/currently.
  c. Once, but not recently.

11. What was your parents' money style when you were growing up?
    a. Minimal control, giving you an extremely generous allowance, access to credit cards, and encouraging you to spend freely just as they did.
    b. Moderate control, giving you a fair allowance and permitting you to spend it mostly as you saw fit (with some possible guidelines).
    c. Tight control, giving you little or no allowance or spending freedom.

12. Which is most important to you when buying a car?
    a. The way it handles.
    b. Good gas mileage.
    c. Its looks.

13. When going out on a major shopping trip, you feel:
    a. Anticipation; you love the thrill of the chase.
    b. Determination; you know just what you need and you intend to find it.
    c. Dread; you hate shopping.

14. Your grocery basket is filled with:
    a. The least expensive items you can find.
    b. Products you love or which save you time (even if they're on the expensive side).
    c. Things you like to eat that aren't too expensive (with occasional splurges).

15. When you're away on vacation, what's your spending style?
    a. Spend as much as you like.
    b. Allot a set amount of money and make sure you confine your spending to this amount, without exception.
    c. Budget some guidelines for spending but retain some flexibility for special purchases and activities.

16. If you had several thousand dollars targeted for investment, you'd be most likely to invest in:
    a. Art, jewelry, Oriental rugs, or other collectibles of investment quality.
    b. A mutual fund that could be liquidated as needed and that would give you some monthly income.
    c. Certificates of deposit (CDs) or bonds that would mature in ten years.

17. You're killing time by browsing in a music store while waiting for a friend to join you at the mall. You see a record/tape/compact disc on sale that looks interesting. What do you do?

    a. Buy the recording on sale as well as another one in case you don't like the first one.

    b. Leave the store and wait outside to avoid temptation, reminding yourself that you hadn't planned on buying anything.

    c. Buy the recording since it's a good price, has gotten good reviews and you haven't bought any music for a while.

SCORING

Total up your points to the seventeen questions as follows.

1. a- 3	b- 5	c- 1
2. a- 5	b- 1	c- 3
3. a- 1	b- 3	c- 5
4. a- 5	b- 1	c- 3
5. a- 5	b- 3	c- 1
6. a- 3	b- 1	c- 5
7. a- 1	b- 3	c- 5
8. a- 5	b- 1	c- 3
9. a- 5	b- 1	c- 3
10. a- 1	b- 5	c- 3
11. a- 5	b- 3	c- 1
12. a- 3	b- 1	c- 5
13. a- 5	b- 3	c- 1
14. a- 1	b- 5	c- 3
15. a- 5	b- 1	c- 3
16. a- 5	b- 3	c- 1
17. a- 5	b- 1	c- 3

17 to 37—saver
38 to 64—user
65 to 85—spender

✳ Profiles

Read on to learn how the way(s) you view and use money can shape your love relationship.

SAVER

As a saver, you're to be commended for your disciplined approach to spending. Instead of just giving in to impulses and whims, you exercise a great deal of self-control in resisting temptation. You're well aware of your financial goals, and you dedicate yourself to achieving them.

In some respects, your money style benefits a love relationship. You and your partner will enjoy the sense of security that comes from living well below your means. You'll make sure your bills and obligations remain at a comfortable level, leaving plenty from your income to save. Getting into debt can place a lot of strain on a relationship, but it's highly unlikely this will ever happen to you.

But your penchant for saving interferes with the full expression and enjoyment of love. Your relationship may be extremely stable, but at a cost. While you'll be spared the lows that occur when spending gets out of control, you're also denying yourself the highs that money can buy. Surprises, fun, romance and adventure are apt to be sorely missing in your life.

When you see the preservation and accumulation of money as an end in itself, you're in trouble. A hefty bank account can bring a certain amount of satisfaction and security, but this has its limits. Concentrating exclusively on building a nest egg for the future means you're ignoring the pleasure that's available in the present.

There's much in life to be treasured that's free, but the economic system we live under dictates that the majority of goods and services comes with a price tag. If you don't want to pay the price (because you find it too high or simply don't want to part with your money), that's your right. And quite often your loss as well. You'll be missing out on a variety of experiences you and your partner could have shared together.

Whether it's dinner at the trendy new restaurant you've heard so much about, a weekend away, redecorating your home, a special play or musical performance or a gift you know your partner would love, money is the resource that enables these things to become a reality rather than a dream.

Pinching pennies and saving can become extremely unhealthy when carried to an extreme. We've all read tales of elderly eccentrics who, although they possessed sizable net worths, scrimped and sacrificed on necessities like food and decent housing. You probably aren't anywhere close to being this fanatical about hoarding your money instead of spending it. But as someone who placed in the quiz's saving category, you need to recognize that your money style leaves much to be desired when it comes to love. The life and love you share with your partner could be significantly enhanced if you loosened the purse strings and allowed your relationship to benefit from the joys money can make possible. For assistance on how to do this, turn to the strategies section on "Using Money to Make Love (and Life) More Special."

USER

You fall in the most desirable category of the three money styles, seeing and using money in a rational, responsible and joyful way. In your perspective, money is to be respected, but not revered. You don't see it as an end-all; it's merely a means for putting pleasure into your life. It enables you to have fun, makes life comfortable, and adds some romantic elements to your relationship. But you'd never go overboard in spending it, nor are you interested in saving as much as possible just for the sake of accumulating it.

Your balanced approach to saving and spending is beneficial to love. You'll make sure you and your partner enjoy nice things and experiences, but never in a way that would compromise your financial stability. You spend only what you can afford because you know that overextending yourself can be highly stressful. While you like material things, you don't feel that anything is worth getting into excessive debt for or believe in working so hard to achieve success and wealth that you don't have time to enjoy it.

Because of your attitude and approach to money, your relationship won't suffer from many financial anxieties. You may not be able to have or do everything you could possibly want, but neither will you be faced with unmanageable bills. You'll reap much satisfaction from your income, putting aside some money for future security while enjoying most of your available resources in the present tense. Unless your partner is an extreme saver or spender, you'll be able to compromise and work out mutually agreeable spending and saving methods.

You're definitely ready for love in terms of being able to use money to support and enhance a relationship. To make sure that you never find yourself in a position of having money compromise your love relationship, you may want to look through the strategies sections just to increase your awareness of techniques for using money in an appropriate way. If you had several answers that fell in the saver category, you'll want to read the section on "Using Money to Make Love (and Life) More Special" to ensure that you never become too much of a saver. Similarly, you'll need to read the section on "Controlling Your Spending so It Doesn't Interfere with Love" if your score was on the upper end of the user scale. (This will help guard against your spending getting out of control.) As long as the majority of your answers were in the user realm, you shouldn't experience many problems combining money with love, but it certainly doesn't hurt to reinforce your money style so it remains positive and healthy over time.

SPENDER

Whereas love can be supported and enhanced by judicious spending, it can be compromised and even destroyed by indiscriminate or uncontrolled spending. If the acquisition and accumulation of products, services and experiences demands all your time/energy/money, you'll be left with very little to share with your partner. Understanding though he or she may be, it can be difficult for someone else to condone your money style. Your partner may eventually refuse to accept the impulsive and usually selfish way you spend money.

For money not to interfere with love, it has to be used in a way that's agreeable to both individuals. It's important to discuss what each person wants and to compromise on some issues. Unfortunately, you're probably not one to discuss money; you like to spend it, not think about it. Nor does compromising come easily to you. You want what you want when you want it and don't relish the thought of denying yourself anything. It's very likely that you'll wind up ignoring your partner's needs while concentrating exclusively on your own.

Especially if carried to an extreme, your spending can impose debt and accompanying anxiety on both you and your partner. You may have little quality time together because you'll be too busy buying and maintaining everything you want to devote much attention to anything but your possessions. By spending every cent you have (and possibly even some you don't have), you won't be doing anything to build a secure future as a couple. Instead, your relationship may be subject to much turbulence should your finances ever take a turn for the worse. Because of your unwillingness to put money aside into savings, you'll experience a great deal of stress in times of high inflation or when an unforeseen event occurs (such as one of you losing your job). This stress can have disastrous consequences for a relationship.

For the sake of your relationship, you won't want to miss the strategies section on "Controlling Your Spending so It Doesn't Interfere with Love." Turn now to this section and learn how you can make some changes in your money style that will improve your ability to love and be loved.

❋ Strategies for Using Money to Support and Enhance Love

Money doesn't have to ruin your relationship. Here's how to make sure it has a positive impact on your love life.

USING MONEY TO MAKE LOVE (AND LIFE) MORE SPECIAL

If you're worried this section is going to demand that you throw caution to the wind and start spending every dime you have on frivolous things, relax. There won't be even subtle suggestions to become a spendthrift. Making a complete reversal in your money style would be counterproductive. It would necessitate fighting your own nature to try to become something you're not. More importantly, unrestrained spending would wreak havoc on your relationship. A balanced approach to saving and spending is crucial for love. All you'll be asked to do is slightly revise your perspective and handling of money.

You need to continue to save money. Being frugal with your finances and setting some aside for future security is something you're an expert at doing and no changes are needed here. What does need addressing is your reluctance to use money to make love and life more special right now. Ask yourself the following questions:

- Do I deserve to enjoy myself now and in the immediate future?
- Does my partner deserve to enjoy himself or herself now and in the immediate future?
- Can money buy things or experiences that will add pleasure to love and life?
- Is it okay to use money to find love and add pleasure to a relationship?

Most likely you answered "yes" to these questions, although you may have been reluctant. If you did not answer every question affirmatively, you may have some deep-rooted problems with money that could benefit from professional counseling. As long as you're able to admit that money can and should be used to enhance your life, you're on your way to being able to use it to support love in a joyful way.

Now you need to determine what areas you've been scrimping on or even totally neglecting. Assuming you haven't been so fanatical about saving that you've denied yourself the basics (adequate food and shelter), your focus will be on those things that can make life and love more fun.

On the worksheet that follows, check off all those items that you feel have potential to add pleasure to your life. Con-

---

✳   ✳

_____ Eating out

_____ Gourmet dinners at home

_____ Short vacation trips (e.g., out-of-town weekends)

_____ Longer vacations (a week or more)

_____ "Dream" vacations (once-in-a-lifetime trips)

_____ Decorating your home

_____ Renovating or improving your home

_____ Buying your dream home

_____ Fresh flowers

_____ Nights on the town (e.g., going dancing or attending plays or concerts)

_____ Surprise "I love you" gifts

_____ Expensive gifts that your partner really wants

_____ Belonging to a health club

_____ Improving your appearance (e.g., extensive hair, skin, makeup treatment at a beauty salon)

_____ Electronics (such as a decent stereo, TV or VCR)

_____ Perfumes or colognes that you enjoy

_____ Overhauling and updating your wardrobe

_____ Participating in activities of your choice (e.g., photography, skiing, flying, jewelry making)

✳   ✳

centrate on those objects or experiences that you've never bought, received or enjoyed, or that have not been a recent part of your life.

Now take a look at the items you checked off. Of these experiences and objects that are currently lacking in your personal world, resolve to introduce some into your life. You may not be able to make any dramatic changes without major revisions in your budget, but you can target a few areas to begin making modest changes. You'll need to spend some money to make them happen, but it will be well worth it. All the areas listed on the worksheet have implications for your love life, either directly (such as enjoying vacations together) or indirectly (increasing your energy level through exercise or your self-esteem by improving your appearance). Some add a sense of romance to your life (e.g., flowers or gifts). None of them can provide you with complete happiness, nor can they fix an ailing relationship, but they can add pleasure to a life or a relationship that is basically satisfactory. Choose three from those you checked off or add some of your own.

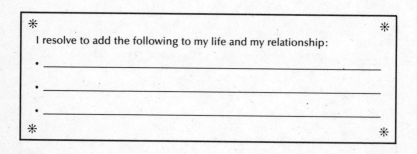

Consider each potential addition individually now and formulate specific goals and financial requirements on the worksheets. Two examples are provided. Each profiles the area to be added, the goal (specifically and objectively stated), steps to take, and the potential cost. After looking at the illustrations, fill out the blank worksheet on your own.

❋   ❋

WHAT I'D LIKE TO ADD TO MY LIFE/MY RELATIONSHIP: Classical music concerts where I can possibly meet the type of man who shares some of my interests.

THE GOAL I'D LIKE TO STRIVE FOR IS . . . attending a concert every month.

ACTION STEP(S) TO REALIZE THE GOAL ARE:
1. Send for literature from the symphony.
2. Set aside five dollars a week for tickets.
3. Select a specific performance and buy tickets.

THE POTENTIAL FINANCIAL IMPLICATIONS OF THIS GOAL ARE: The cost of a ticket (about $20/month).

❋   ❋

❋   ❋

WHAT I'D LIKE TO ADD TO MY LIFE/MY RELATIONSHIP: Getting myself in better shape to be more attractive for my partner.

THE GOAL I'D LIKE TO STRIVE FOR IS: Working out three times a week.

ACTION STEP(S) TO REALIZE THE GOAL ARE:
1. Check out a few health clubs.
2. Arrange to exercise three times a week.

THE POTENTIAL FINANCIAL IMPLICATIONS OF THIS GOAL ARE: The cost of health club membership.

❋   ❋

✳   ✳

WHAT I'D LIKE TO ADD TO MY LIFE/MY RELATIONSHIP:

_____

_____

THE GOAL I'D LIKE TO STRIVE FOR IS: _____

_____

_____

ACTION STEP(S) TO REALIZE THIS GOAL ARE:

_____

_____

THE POTENTIAL FINANCIAL IMPLICATIONS OF THIS GOAL ARE:

_____

_____

_____

✳   ✳

In filling out the worksheet, you've made a commitment in writing to spend some money to add more satisfaction to love and life. But don't stop there. You should also work on setting aside some funds for spontaneous spending. This money should be used however you want when you want, but the emphasis should be on using it on a regular basis to buy special things or experiences for you and your (present or

✳   ✳

Amount of money to be spent each month to make love and life more special:

$_____

✳   ✳

future) partner. Decide how much you'd like to target on a monthly basis and be sure you use and enjoy these funds. Avoid the temptation to revert to your usual mode and sock it away. Even if it's uncomfortable at first, force yourself to spend this money in a pleasurable way.

CONTROLLING YOUR SPENDING SO IT DOESN'T INTERFERE WITH LOVE

If you flipped through the preceding pages before you came to this section, you were probably amazed to see that some people need encouragement or advice on how to spend money. This is definitely not your problem. You're well versed in spending money. It comes easily and naturally to you. And this isn't necessarily a negative characteristic. As long as you enjoy what you buy and live within your means, you don't need to be concerned.

But things often get out of control for spenders. If your thirst for new objects to possess and expensive activities to participate in is unquenchable, you may find yourself heavily in debt one day. If you misperceive your wants as needs and feel they must be satisfied at all costs, you're likely to spend more than you can afford. An inordinate amount of stress can be placed on a relationship when this occurs. Because an irresponsible and uncontrolled spending pattern can interfere with your ability to love and be loved, you need to recognize when your spending has become a problem.

Be truthful in answering these questions. Your money style may not be something you're especially proud of, but it's crucial you own up to how and why you tend to overspend.

- Do I feel I deserve whatever I want and therefore make sure I always get it, regardless of the cost?
- Do I resent having to deny myself anything?
- Do I experience a rush of excitement when I buy something?
- Is this the only excitement I have in my life?
- Do I prefer to spend my money without any thought or planning as to how it will be used?
- Do I feel better about myself when I spend money and acquire the latest or most expensive things?

An affirmative answer to any of these questions indicates the potential for a spending problem that can interfere with love. Read on if you had even one "yes."

There's certainly no right or wrong way to spend money. Your spending patterns will reflect your own unique needs and wants. As a spender, you tend to spend money without giving much thought to it. It's highly unlikely that you know exactly how you're spending it. (Only a real saver can account for every penny!) You probably also feel your spending is justifiable for the most part because your purchases save you time/energy or give you pleasure. But you also may suspect there are areas in which you overspend. Read the following list and check off those items where you spend more money than you really should. Keep in mind the proportion of your income you're spending on each area as well as your actual spending habits (e.g., whether you attempt to cut costs by comparison shopping, waiting for sales and so on).

✳   ✳

_____ Groceries

_____ Meals at restaurants

_____ Alcohol (at home or out)

_____ Clothes and accessories

_____ Cosmetics/grooming products

_____ Grooming (hair, skin and nail care)

_____ Exercise/sports

_____ Automobile and related expenses

_____ Travel/vacations

_____ Mortgage or rent payments

_____ Home decorating

_____ Electronics (computer, video and audio equipment; supplies such as records and tapes; gadgets for the home or for personal use)

_____ Entertaining at home

_____ Gifts

_____ Going out (movies, concerts, etc.)

_____ Leisure activities (e.g., hobbies)

_____ Services (such as house or car cleaning)

_____ Pets

_____ Expenses for your child (such as private school)

_____ Reading material (books, newspaper/magazine subscriptions)

_____ Gambling (including lottery tickets)

You're not necessarily in trouble just because you checked off a couple of items. It's possible to overspend in a particular area and underspend in another. The list will help you balance things so your spending doesn't ruin your financial or romantic well-being. But if there are many areas where you spend more than you should, you need to consider what modifications are called for. You're certainly entitled to spend money on things that make you happy, but only in an appropriate way. Spending more than you can afford will quickly catch up with you and cause inordinate amounts of stress for both you and your partner.

A pattern of reckless spending may have brought you some short-term pleasure, but in the long run it can only cause major difficulties in your life. You need to learn to use money in a responsible way that will provide enjoyment for you and the person you love most. Until you win the lottery or discover an unknown but very rich relative who died and left you a fortune, you'll have to adjust your spending habits to reflect the limitations your income imposes. Decide where you want to begin to control your spending. Choose three areas from those you checked off or add some of your own.

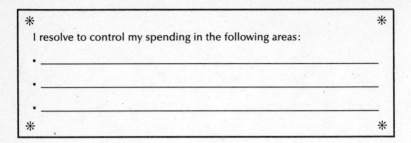

```
  *                                              *
    I resolve to control my spending in the following areas:

    • _____

    • _____

    • _____
  *                                              *
```

It's beyond the scope of this book to show you specific methods for controlling your spending. But there are many books and magazines that can help you do this. Read as many as it takes to understand your spending patterns and where you're going wrong. Consult more frugal family and friends about how they spend/save money and consider their suggestions for how you could do better in this area. If charge cards present problems, seek consumer/credit counseling. In extreme cases, a credit counselor will advise destroying all charge cards and paying cash for all purposes.

Now decide how you're going to curb some of your excessive spending. Determine what you want to spend in each of the three areas you targeted on the previous worksheet. After reading the three examples, you can fill in your own worksheet with one of your targeted areas, the limit of money to be spent and ways to spend less in this area.

```
  *                                              *
    I NEED TO SPEND LESS ON: food.

    MY LIMIT FOR THIS AREA IS: $240 per month.

    WAYS TO SPEND LESS IN THIS AREA ARE:
    1. Use convenience foods less; cook from scratch.
    2. Use coupons.
    3. Start a series of dinner parties with friends instead of going out to eat.
  *                                              *
```

✳   ✳

I NEED TO SPEND LESS ON: Car expenses.

MY LIMIT FOR THIS AREA IS: $300 per month.

WAYS TO SPEND LESS IN THIS AREA ARE:
1. Consider car pooling.
2. Shop around for a cheaper car.
3. Learn to do your own minor repairs and maintenance.

✳   ✳

✳   ✳

I NEED TO SPEND LESS ON: Utilities.

MY LIMIT FOR THIS AREA IS: $125 per month.

WAYS TO SPEND LESS IN THIS AREA ARE:
1. Write letters to out-of-state friends and family instead of making so many long-distance calls.
2. Investigate energy-efficient ways to heat/cool home (e.g., ceiling fans, water heater switch and cover, resetting the thermostat a little higher in summer and lower in winter).

✳   ✳

✳   ✳

I NEED TO SPEND LESS ON: _____

_____

MY LIMIT FOR THIS AREA IS: _____

_____

WAYS TO SPEND LESS IN THIS AREA ARE:

_____

_____

_____

_____

✳   ✳

Learning to live within your budget will take a lot of effort at first, but eventually it will become second nature to you. You and the partner who shares your life now or in the future will enjoy the increased security and peace of mind your new approach will bring. An additional reward can be the opportunity to save for big purchases you both want, such as an upgraded home or a special vacation. It's certainly okay to use your money—you just need to make sure not to spend it in a reckless way that interferes with love. If you can keep love from "burning a hole" in your pocket, you'll be able to prevent it from burning holes in your relationship.

RECOMMENDED READING

Felton-Collins, Victoria. *Couples and Money.* New York: Bantam Books, 1990.

Gurney, Kathleen. *Your Money Personality.* New York: Doubleday, 1988.

Hallowell, Edward, M., and William J. Grace. *What Are You Worth?* New York: Weidenfeld and Nicholson, 1989.

Lieberman, Annette, and Vicki Lindner. *Unbalanced Accounts.* New York: Atlantic Monthly Press, 1987.

Porter, Sylvia. *Love and Money.* New York: Morrow, 1985.

Weinstein, Grace W. *Men, Women, and Money.* New York: New American Library, 1986.

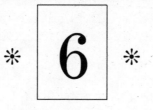

❋ **6** ❋

Can You Give and Receive Sexual Pleasure?

Sex is not the only (nor is it the major) element that binds two people together in a love relationship, but it *is* an important means of expressing affection and receiving gratification. It's one of the many benefits of loving someone and being loved by that person. In an ideal love relationship, both partners derive significant emotional and physical satisfaction from their sexual activity.

But satisfying sex does not automatically accompany love. Although a couple may care deeply about each other, one or both partners may experience less than optimal fulfillment in the sex life they share. These problems usually aren't confined to the sexual area; their impact is felt in most aspects of a relationship.

For sex really to work in a relationship, each partner needs to be able both to give and receive pleasure. The quiz in this chapter will enable you to determine just where you stand in these two abilities. If, like many people, you have not fully developed your ability to either give or receive sexual pleasure, the strategies section will offer some suggestions on how to increase your expertise in the appropriate area.

✳   # QUIZ   ✳

The following quiz is not intended to measure your sexual performance skills. Sexual acrobatics, in and of themselves, are ultimately meaningless. What's far more important is your ability to give and receive pleasure. Keeping this in mind, rate yourself honestly on the characteristics and traits below.

Assign ratings to each of the areas in Part A by circling the number that best describes your typical functioning with the partner(s) you've had in the past or the one you're currently with. The scoring ranges from a low of 1 to a high of 10. For example, if you feel you have excellent knowledge of your partner's anatomy and physiology, you might rate yourself as an 8, 9 or even a 10 in this area. If, on the other hand, you feel that your knowledge of your partner's genitals is limited to the basics, circle a score from 3 to 5.

Once you finish Part A, go on to Part B and circle your responses. Scoring should be completely independent of that which you assigned for Part A; do not refer back to the first part to compare your scores with Part B.

Part A

Circle the number (1 is the lowest and 10 is the highest) that approximates your skills and traits in each area.

1. My knowledge of what gives my partner pleasure (in terms of sexual conditions such as times, places, sounds, smells and sexual techniques).
   1 2 3 4 5 6 7 8 9 10

2. My knowledge of my partner's anatomy and physiology.
   1 2 3 4 5 6 7 8 9 10

3. My comfort level with my partner's anatomy and physiology.
   1 2 3 4 5 6 7 8 9 10

4. The likelihood of my seeing a sex therapist if my partner were having sexual problems.
   1 2 3 4 5 6 7 8 9 10

5. My ability to encourage my partner to express his or her sexual needs.
   1 2 3 4 5 6 7 8 9 10

6. The typical energy I expend in giving my partner an orgasm.
   1 2 3 4 5 6 7 8 9 10

7. The amount of time and effort I devote to pleasuring my partner without directly trying to bring him or her to orgasm (e.g., foreplay and afterplay such as kissing, fondling and massage, which doesn't involve the goal of climax).
   1 2 3 4 5 6 7 8 9 10

8. The likelihood of my initiating sexual activity when I sense my partner desires it.
   1 2 3 4 5 6 7 8 9 10

9. My ability to help my partner feel relaxed, both in and out of the bedroom.
   1 2 3 4 5 6 7 8 9 10

10. My ability to make my partner feel attractive, desirable, and cherished, not just during sex but in general.
    1 2 3 4 5 6 7 8 9 10

Part B

Circle the number (1 is the lowest and 10 is the highest) that approximates your skills and traits in each area.

1. My awareness of what gives me pleasure (in terms of sexual conditions such as times, places, sounds, smells, tastes and sexual techniques).
   1 2 3 4 5 6 7 8 9 10

2. My knowledge of my own anatomy and physiology.
   1 2 3 4 5 6 7 8 9 10

3. My comfort level with my own anatomy and physiology.
   1 2 3 4 5 6 7 8 9 10

4. The likelihood of my seeing a sex therapist if I were having sexual problems.
   1   2   3   4   5   6   7   8   9   10

5. My ability to express my sexual needs to my partner.
   1   2   3   4   5   6   7   8   9   10

6. The typical energy I expend in ensuring that I have an orgasm.
   1   2   3   4   5   6   7   8   9   10

7. The amount of time and effort my partner and/or I devote to pleasuring me without directly trying to bring me to orgasm (e.g., foreplay and afterplay such as kissing, fondling and massage, which doesn't involve the goal of climax).
   1   2   3   4   5   6   7   8   9   10

8. The likelihood of my initiating sexual activity when I desire it.
   1   2   3   4   5   6   7   8   9   10

9. My ability to feel relaxed, both in and out of the bedroom.
   1   2   3   4   5   6   7   8   9   10

10. My perception of myself as an attractive and desirable person, not just during sex but all the time.
    1   2   3   4   5   6   7   8   9   10

SCORING

Add up the numbers you circled in Part A. If, for example, you circled one 10, one 9, three 8's, four 7's, and one 4, your total score would be 75 ($10+9+8+8+8+7+7+7+7+4$). Record your score below.

Do the same for Part B.

A _____
B _____

If your scores for A and B are very similar (within three points), you can consider yourself to be both a giver and receiver of sexual pleasure. The "Giver—Receiver" profile describes your sexual style.

But if your A score is more than three points higher than your B score (e.g., 84 for A and 77 for B), you're more of a giver than a receiver and should consult the "Giver" profile that follows.

If your B score is more than three points higher than your A score (e.g., 93 for B and 88 for A), this indicates a greater tendency toward receiving sexual pleasure than giving it. You need to read the "Receiver" profile in the next section.

✳ Profiles

Find the profile that corresponds to the score you received in the quiz.

GIVER

You're a generous partner in the bedroom (and probably outside as well). You don't just make claims about pleasing your partner. Instead, you expend considerable effort making him or her happy. Your physical and mental energies are devoted to your partner's satisfaction, even at the expense of your own. Your goal is to provide pleasure for the person you love, not obtain it for yourself. This sexual altruism may come naturally to you, without any thought or planning. As a giver, it's unlikely that you perceive your actions as a sacrifice. You're only too glad to do it for your partner.

The ideal partner for you is one who appreciates your giving nature. He or she needs to be aware of how much you care and all you do to express that love. If he or she tends to be a giver, too, your efforts may be reciprocated. A thoughtless or selfish partner could easily take advantage of you and never consider your sexual needs or desires.

If your partner gives as much to you as you do to him or her, the two of you will be in good shape. But this scenario is all too rare in reality. Givers often choose partners who excel at taking rather than giving. Opposites attract here because the taker needs someone to take from and the giver needs a person who will receive the gifts he or she wants to offer. The chances of your being paired with someone who's as giving as you are slim. More than likely, you'll find yourself with a partner who does not give back nearly as much as he or she receives and enjoys from you.

On the surface, a relationship where one partner wants to give and the other to receive would seem to work for both individuals. But this is not always the case. A one-sided relationship may eventually take its toll on both the giver and the receiver. Your giving nature has some limits. There may be a point at which you're no longer happy to give without receiv-

ing something in return. You may start resenting your partner, and this will not be healthy for your relationship.

Unless your partner is a totally uncaring and selfish person, he or she may experience some feelings of guilt about all
your constant giving. Like resentment, guilt is not an emotion
that is conducive to satisfying sex for either partner, nor is it
an appropriate foundation for the nonsexual ways you relate to
each other. If guilt or a sense of duty is the only thing motivat-
ing your partner to reciprocate your efforts, his or her attempts at giving you pleasure will be feeble at best. Ultimately, neither of you will wind up enjoying sex as much as
you could.

When you don't put sufficient effort into making sex pleasurable for you as well as your partner, you both will be
shortchanged. You'll be depriving yourself of the physical and
emotional rewards that sex can offer. Similarly, you'll be preventing your partner from the enjoyment of sharing sex with a
responsive lover who realizes that real lovemaking entails
mutual satisfaction.

Even if you've been a giver for most of your life, it's still
possible to learn how to be on the receiving end, too. You can
continue to be a generous sexual partner while looking out for
yourself and making sure that you obtain satisfaction. Turn
now to the "Receiving More Sexual Pleasure" discussion in the
strategies section for more information on the subject.

GIVER-RECEIVER

You appear to be ideally balanced in the sexual arena. As
both a giver and receiver, you experience the best of both
worlds. By ensuring that sex is gratifying for you and your
partner, you can reap the full rewards of lovemaking.

As far as sex is concerned, you can consider yourself ready
for love. But this doesn't necessarily mean you've reached
your full potential as a sexual being. You can always acquire
more knowledge and develop new skills that will further enhance physical love for both you and your partner. Be sure to
read both "Giving More Sexual Pleasure" and "Receiving
More Sexual Pleasure" in the strategies section to maximize
your functioning in both these crucial areas.

RECEIVER

If you're squirming in discomfort because you landed in this category, stop right now. There's absolutely no shame in taking an active role in ensuring your own sexual pleasure. Your approach is basically a healthy one. You realize that the responsibility for sexual fulfillment rests with yourself. It's up to you (not your partner) to make sure that sex is satisfying for you.

Most people would enjoy having sex with you because you're so involved in lovemaking. Your sexual energy and interest make you a much more exciting partner than someone who is passive and apathetic in bedroom activities. Unlike other individuals who may worry that their lovers are engaging in sex only as an obligation or duty, your partner never has to question your motives. It's obvious that you have sex because it gives you pleasure.

Having a lover who feels so positively about sex can do a lot for your partner's ego. He or she will feel attractive, desirable and sexually competent. Your partner won't be bothered by the self-doubts and anxieties that arise when a mate is disinterested or unsatisfied.

If you were passive or reluctant about your needs and desires, your partner would have to spend considerable effort helping you enjoy sex more. Your ability to obtain sexual pleasure gives your partner the freedom to concentrate on his or her own fulfillment. This sexual assertiveness increases the likelihood of your mutual satisfaction.

But if you focus exclusively on your own pleasure, you'll be missing out on the joy of giving pleasure to the person you love. Satisfying sex isn't as simple as each partner fulfilling his or her own needs. It's the sharing and caring that carries sex in a love relationship far beyond a mere physiological activity.

There are a variety of reasons why people strive to provide pleasure for their partners. Sometimes the motivation stems from a need to gain or retain the partner's interest. It may reflect an attempt to repay the partner for his or her generosity or commitment. At times, it's a peace offering to make up for angry words or hurtful actions. Occasionally, it may arise from a need to feel sexually attractive and skilled. You may have pleasured your partner in the past or will pleasure him or her in the future for any or all of these reasons.

It's quite possible for your partner to enjoy sex regardless of the reason(s) you engage in it. But you will be denying him or her the emotional satisfaction that comes from having a partner who provides sexual pleasure as a means of expressing love. All the other reasons can be traced to simple self-interest. When you give only for the purpose of getting in return, you're not giving (and your partner is not receiving) love in its purest form.

As you read "Giving More Sexual Pleasure" in the strategies section, you'll be shifting your focus to your partner's wants and needs. By acquiring the knowledge and skill to understand and deliver what will make your partner happy, you'll be more ready for the give and take of sexual love.

✳ Strategies for Enhancing Sex

Although you'll want to concentrate on "Receiving More Sexual Pleasure" if you're a giver and "Giving More Sexual Pleasure" if you're a receiver, it can be helpful to read both sections so you can develop an optimally balanced approach to sex.

RECEIVING MORE SEXUAL PLEASURE

Loving someone doesn't mean that you have to concentrate exclusively on his or her pleasure while neglecting your own needs and desires. If your partner truly loves you, he or she wants sex to be equally enjoyable for you. Satisfying sex is also something you should want for yourself.

Both you and your partner need to know exactly what you like and dislike in sexual activities and conditions. You probably have some general ideas about your sexual preferences, but you may never have delineated any specifics. Your partner won't know what it is you want when you lack this knowledge about yourself.

It's imperative that you learn all you can about your sexuality. Read some of the books recommended at the end of this chapter to gain a better understanding of your sexual anatomy and physiology. While you undoubtedly know the basics, there's always something you can learn that will enhance your awareness and appreciation of your sexual functioning. Be sure to learn about things that can adversely affect your ability to want and receive sexual pleasure. Excessive stress, alcohol, nicotine and drugs such as antidepressants, tranquilizers and even antihistamines for colds or allergies can negatively impact upon your ability to enjoy sex.

If you're currently without a partner, you can learn to pleasure yourself. By doing so, you'll be acquiring vital information that you can later convey to the person you love. If you're in a relationship, have your partner experiment with a variety of techniques, styles and conditions to increase your awareness of what you like and what you don't.

Use the worksheets that follow to pinpoint your awareness of your own preferences. You can base your answers on what you've enjoyed in the past if you're not sexually active at this time. If you're in a love relationship now, base your answers on your sexual experiences with this partner.

✻   ✻

Every individual has his or her unique sexual preferences. For each of the following sexual activities, put a " + " in the blank if you like it, a " − " if you do not like it, and a "?" if you're not sure.

_____ Hugging

_____ Light kissing

_____ Deep ("French") kissing

_____ Having neck, stomach, back, buttocks, arms, fingers, legs, or toes kissed

_____ Having ears nibbled

_____ Having face or body licked

_____ Receiving a massage

_____ Having thighs stroked

_____ Having genitals manually stimulated

_____ Receiving oral stimulation of genitals

_____ Receiving anal stimulation

_____ Being on top during intercourse

_____ Being on bottom during intercourse

_____ Acting out fantasies

_____ Showering or bathing together

_____ Reading sexually explicit material

_____ Viewing sexually explicit photos or films

_____ Talking "dirty" or hearing partner talk "dirty"

_____ Extensive foreplay

_____ Extensive afterplay

_____ Lengthy sexual encounters

✳   ✳

✳   ✳

People enjoy sex under a variety of circumstances and environmental factors. For each of the following sexual conditions, write down your specific preferences.

SENSORY STIMULATION

Auditory (e.g., music such as rock, classical, jazz or country; minimal talking; lots of talking, talking "dirty"; laughter; noises such as sighing, moaning, screaming, heavy breathing):

_____

_____

_____

_____

Visual (e.g., total darkness, bright lights, candlelight):

_____

_____

_____

_____

Tactile (e.g., satin sheets, silk underwear, massage creams and lotions):

_____

_____

_____

_____

Gustatory (e.g., flavored/edible oils, lotions or condoms; liquor or food consumed during sex):

_____

_____

_____

_____

Olfactory (e.g., scented candles, room deodorizers, perfumes and colognes):

_____

_____

_____

_____

WHERE AND WHEN

Time (e.g., morning, evening, before bed):

_____

_____

_____

_____

Place (e.g., bedroom, living room, outdoors):

_____

_____

_____

_____

HOW

Mood (e.g., playful, romantic, leisurely, rushed):

_____

_____

_____

_____

Beginnings (e.g., extended foreplay, spontaneous sex):

_____

_____

_____

_____

Endings (e.g., extended afterplay, eating, drinking, smoking, falling asleep after sex):

_____

_____

_____

_____

❊   ❊

If any of the questions proves difficult to answer, both you and your partner could be in trouble. Your partner will be frustrated because he or she won't know how to satisfy you, and you'll be unhappy with a partner who can't provide you with the type of sex you want. You'll be doing both of you a favor to learn all you can about yourself.

Once you know what you want sexually, the next step is to convey this information to your partner. It may be helpful to show him or her the two worksheets you've completed, since these quickly and easily spell out your preferences. But don't expect the worksheets to do the entire job for you. They can supplement your verbal and nonverbal communication, but they should not be used as a substitute for the in-depth sharing of your thoughts and feelings.

Ideally, you should both show and tell your partner what you like. By placing your partner's hand where you want it or demonstrating the pressure or pace you desire, there will be no doubt about what gives you pleasure. You also need to communicate verbally. Tell your partner exactly what you enjoy and what you want. Don't ask for things that are vague, such as "more affection"; make your requests specific (e.g., cuddling after sex). Be careful not to blame or belittle your partner for not doing something correctly. Instead of criticizing his or her actions, focus on your preferences. For example, don't accuse your partner of going too fast; simply note that you prefer a slow, relaxed pace.

✳   ✳

Place an X by all items that reflect your feelings about your looks.

_____ Too thin

_____ Too heavy

_____ Not muscular or toned enough

_____ Too tall

_____ Too short

_____ Face not attractive enough

_____ Hair not styled well

_____ Breasts too small

_____ Breasts too large

_____ Breasts uneven in size

_____ Shoulders/chest/arms underdeveloped or flabby

_____ Stomach flabby

_____ Hips too large

_____ Hips too small

_____ Legs not shapely or developed enough

_____ Buttocks too small

_____ Buttocks too big

_____ Too hairy

_____ Not hairy enough

_____ Not well groomed enough

_____ Not sufficiently well dressed

Now place another X by those items that have a negative impact upon your own or your partner's sexual pleasure. Base your responses on a love relationship with a past, present or future partner who cares about the total you.

✳   ✳

But ultimately, the responsibility for obtaining sexual pleasure rests with you. While your partner can help provide you with the physical and emotional atmosphere that is conducive to your mutual enjoyment, it's up to you to enable yourself to derive satisfaction from sex.

One crucial element in enjoying sex is self-acceptance. If you're uncomfortable or unhappy with yourself for any reason, your ability to receive sexual pleasure will be diminished. Worrying about your looks interferes with your sexual desire and responsiveness. No matter how affectionate and giving your partner is, his or her efforts will be in vain if you feel unattractive and, consequently, not worthy or deserving of happiness.

Use the worksheet that follows to pinpoint your feelings about your sexual attractiveness.

Chances are you found several items on the worksheet that

you feel pertain to real or imaginary deficiencies in your looks. Most people are not completely happy with the way they look and wish they could change some things about their features or physique. In reality, none of the listed "problems" should decrease pleasure for either of you. Men and women of all shapes and sizes enjoy sex with each other. But if you found one or more items that you feel interferes with your partner's or your own pleasure, you need to recognize that it's your perception of yourself as undesirable (rather than your actual "flaws") that prevents you (and your partner) from getting the most out of sex.

You can work at improving your appearance through dieting, exercise or even plastic surgery. Keeping yourself in great shape will do a lot for your self-confidence and will make you feel more comfortable with yourself as a sexual being. But because genetics determines such a large part of facial and body features, it's fruitless to try to remake yourself into something you're not and can't ever be. Far more important to your psychosexual well-being is learning to accept yourself as you are.

Do whatever it takes to come to terms with who you are. Learn to appreciate your appearance and personality instead of focusing on flaws. There are many books available that can help you to feel more positive about yourself. Join a self-help group that will enable you to share your feelings and develop strategies for increasing your self-worth. Obtain professional counseling if needed. Try to get to the point where you no longer feel that any of the items on the previous worksheet has any real implications for receiving or giving sexual love.

Always remember that sex has as much to do with the mind as it does with the body. If, while growing up, you were given negative messages about sexual pleasure, you may still be retaining subconscious thoughts and feelings that work against your enjoyment. As an impressionable child it is close to impossible not to incorporate these messages from family and religious instruction into your psyche; but as an adult you can deal with them more effectively and discard those that aren't healthy for you. Again, there are many books, support groups and therapists to help you develop improved attitudes about sex.

Specific techniques that can be used to increase your ability to receive sexual pleasure are:

- Repeating positive affirmations such as "I'm loved and desired by my partner. I deserve to enjoy myself sexually and every other way with the person I love."

  By telling yourself these things before and during sex, you'll be more receptive to obtaining pleasure.

- Visualizing yourself enjoying sex.

  Create a movie in your mind where you're both the star and director. The subject: your sexual pleasure. Once you "see" yourself pursuing and receiving satisfying sex, it will be easier to make it happen in reality.

- Fantasizing about whatever it is that will make sex great for you.

  You can share your fantasies with your partner and both act them out, or you can keep them to yourself for your own enjoyment prior to or during sex.

- Setting an optimal mood for sex.

  On the worksheet you completed at the beginning of this section, you recorded specific conditions that make sex most pleasurable for you. If these conditions are ignored, you'll be less likely to enjoy yourself during lovemaking. Be sure to establish these conditions whenever possible so you'll receive maximum pleasure. Also keep in mind that stress is usually not conducive to your sexual enjoyment. Learn ways to reduce excessive stress in your life and to cope with the stresses you can't do anything about.

Make a commitment now to do something to increase your ability to receive sexual pleasure. The worksheet that follows illustrates concrete plans to improve your sexual fulfillment. Complete the blank worksheet by choosing one or more items to focus on, and then take action. You owe it to yourself to put some energy into this important area of life and love.

✳   ✳

I RESOLVE TO DO THE FOLLOWING TO IMPROVE MY ABILITY TO RECEIVE SEXUAL PLEASURE:

__X__ LEARNING MORE ABOUT MY SEXUALITY IN TERMS OF: The cycles of my sexual desire.

TO ACCOMPLISH THIS, I WILL: Read two books on the subject.

__X__ COMMUNICATE MY SEXUAL NEEDS AND WANTS TO MY PARTNER, SUCH AS: My desire for at least twenty minutes of foreplay.

TO ACCOMPLISH THIS, I WILL: Bring this up for discussion after dinner when we're both relaxed.

__X__ ACCEPTING MYSELF, INCLUDING MY FLAWS SUCH AS: My "thunder thighs."

TO ACCOMPLISH THIS, I WILL: Exercise to tone them as much as possible, but I won't allow myself to dwell on them.

__X__ INCORPORATE POSITIVE AFFIRMATIONS ABOUT MYSELF AND MY SEXUALITY.

TO ACCOMPLISH THIS, I WILL TELL MYSELF THAT: I'm a great person with many talents, including lovemaking.

__X__ VISUALIZE MYSELF ENJOYING SEX.

TO ACCOMPLISH THIS, I WILL PICTURE MYSELF: Enjoying a sensual back rub that eventually leads to other things.

__X__ FANTASIZE TO MAXIMIZE MY PLEASURE.

TO ACCOMPLISH THIS, I WILL THINK ABOUT OR ACT OUT THE FANTASY OF: Having sex with a stranger with whom there's an intense and instant mutual attraction.

__X__ ENSURE THAT THE MOOD AND ATMOSPHERE IS CONDUCIVE TO MY SEXUAL PLEASURE.

TO ACCOMPLISH THIS, I WILL MAKE SURE THAT: The lights are turned low and we start making love before I get too tired to enjoy it (e.g., before ten).

✳   ✳

✳   ✳

I RESOLVE TO DO THE FOLLOWING TO IMPROVE MY ABILITY TO
RECEIVE SEXUAL PLEASURE:

——————— LEARN MORE ABOUT MY SEXUALITY IN TERMS OF: ———

    TO ACCOMPLISH THIS, I WILL: ——————————————

    ——————————————————————————————————

    ——————————————————————————————————

——————— COMMUNICATE MY SEXUAL NEEDS TO MY PARTNER,
    SUCH AS: ———————————————————————————

    TO ACCOMPLISH THIS, I WILL: ——————————————

    ——————————————————————————————————

    ——————————————————————————————————

——————— ACCEPT MYSELF, INCLUDING MY FLAWS SUCH AS: ———

    TO ACCOMPLISH THIS, I WILL: ——————————————

    ——————————————————————————————————

    ——————————————————————————————————

——————— INCORPORATE POSITIVE AFFIRMATIONS ABOUT MYSELF
    AND MY SEXUALITY.

    TO ACCOMPLISH THIS, I WILL TELL MYSELF THAT:

    ——————————————————————————————————

    ——————————————————————————————————

——————— VISUALIZE MYSELF ENJOYING SEX.

    TO ACCOMPLISH THIS, I WILL PICTURE MYSELF:

    ——————————————————————————————————

    ——————————————————————————————————

——————— FANTASIZE TO MAXIMIZE MY PLEASURE.

    TO ACCOMPLISH THIS, I WILL THINK ABOUT OR ACT
    OUT THE FANTASY OF: ————————————————————

    ——————————————————————————————————

    ——————————————————————————————————

_____ ENSURE THAT THE MOOD AND ATMOSPHERE IS
CONDUCIVE TO MY SEXUAL PLEASURE.

TO ACCOMPLISH THIS, I WILL: _____

_____

_____

*   *

GIVING MORE SEXUAL PLEASURE

Don't let the heading of this section scare you. You're not totally responsible for your partner's sexual enjoyment. In fact, you really can't "give" your partner an orgasm or make him or her feel good about sex. It's up to him or her to develop the attitude and skills that make sex pleasurable. He or she also needs to invest considerable mental and physical energy to ensure that sex is personally fulfilling.

Although you're not ultimately responsible for your partner's happiness in and out of the bedroom, it's important for both your sakes that you expend some effort into giving him or her pleasure. Your partner wants to feel you care enough to focus on some of his or her needs. Sex provides a very tangible way for you to express your love. It allows you to demonstrate your interest in your partner and your appreciation of him or her. By doing this, you enable yourself to experience the satisfaction of moving away from your own concerns and needs as you concentrate instead on doing something nice for your partner.

The key element in giving your partner pleasure is communication. It's essential that you know exactly what your partner likes (and dislikes). Because you're not a mind reader, the only accurate way to obtain this information is to ask him or her. Nonverbal clues during sex will also shed some light on what your partner prefers during lovemaking, but body language, facial expressions, and noises can often be difficult to read. Open discussion is the most efficient and loving method of learning about your partner's sexual needs.

Many of us feel more comfortable performing sexual activity than we do talking about it. If this is true for you, it will take some courage and determination to initiate these intimate conversations. Your partner may be similarly reticent about discussing his or her sexual preferences. You may need to proceed gradually until you both feel more at ease. Little by little, you'll discover that sharing your thoughts and feelings about sex isn't nearly as embarrassing or threatening as you had anticipated.

To communicate well about sex, you'll need to become a good listener. If your partner finds it difficult to discuss sex freely, you can start by talking about your own needs and asking how his or hers compare with yours. Listen attentively and then repeat what you believe you've heard to make sure you've understood.

Accept what your partner tells you. You may not agree with or like everything he or she has to say, but don't pass any value judgments. Remember that your partner is as entitled to his or her preferences as you are to yours. If you attack or criticize them, your partner will be less likely to discuss sexual (and possibly nonsexual) issues candidly in the future.

Be sure to acquire specific information about your partner's preferences. Vague generalities will not offer much guidance. You need to know exactly what your partner finds pleasing and what he or she does not. If you don't know what your partner likes, you won't be able to give it to him or her.

The worksheets that follow will enable you to check your awareness of your partner's preferences. If you're not currently involved with someone, you can base your answers on a past partner so you can see whether or not you had sufficient information about your lover to make him or her happy. If you're in a relationship now, evaluate your knowledge of your partner's likes and dislikes. Should any of the items prove difficult to answer because you never discussed or tried them with your partner, you'll need to learn more about your partner's feelings toward the activity or condition in question. You cannot consider yourself totally ready for love until you're well aware of your partner's needs and desires.

✻   ✻

Every individual has his or her unique sexual preferences. For each of the following sexual activities, put a "+" in the blank if your partner (past or present) likes it, a "−" if he or she does not like it, and a "?" if you're not sure.

_____ Hugging

_____ Light kissing

_____ Deep ("French") kissing

_____ Having neck, stomach, back, buttocks, arms, fingers, legs, or toes kissed

_____ Having ears nibbled

_____ Having face or body licked

_____ Receiving a massage

_____ Having thighs stroked

_____ Having genitals manually stimulated

_____ Receiving oral stimulation of genitals

_____ Receiving anal stimulation

_____ Being on top during intercourse

_____ Being on bottom during intercourse

_____ Acting out fantasies

_____ Showering or bathing together

_____ Reading sexually explicit material

_____ Viewing sexually explicit photos or films

_____ Talking "dirty" or hearing partner talk "dirty"

_____ Extensive foreplay

_____ Extensive afterplay

_____ Lengthy sexual encounters

✻   ✻

✳   ✳

People enjoy sex under a variety of circumstances and environmental factors. For each of the following sexual conditions, write down your partner's typical preferences. Be as specific as possible.

SENSORY STIMULATION

Auditory (e.g., music such as rock, classical, jazz, or country; minimal talking; lots of talking; talking "dirty"; laughter; noises such as sighing, moaning, screaming, heavy breathing):

_____

_____

_____

_____

Visual (e.g., total darkness, bright lights, candlelight):

_____

_____

_____

Tactile (e.g., satin sheets, silk underwear, massage creams and lotions):

_____

_____

_____

_____

Gustatory (e.g., flavored/edible oils, lotions, or condoms; liquor or food consumed during sex):

_____

_____

_____

_____

Olfactory (e.g., scented candles; room deodorizers; perfumes and colognes):

_____

_____

_____

_____

WHERE AND WHEN

Time (e.g., morning, evening, before bed):

_____

_____

_____

_____

Place (e.g., bedroom, living room, outdoors):

_____

_____

_____

_____

HOW

Mood (e.g., playful, romantic, leisurely, rushed):

_____

_____

_____

_____

Beginnings (e.g., extended foreplay, spontaneous sex):

_____

_____

_____

_____

Endings (e.g., extended afterplay, eating, drinking, smoking, falling asleep after sex):

_____

_____

_____

_____

✳   ✳

In addition to knowing your partner's likes and dislikes, it's also important that you have a thorough knowledge of his or her sexual anatomy and physiology. Unless you've been fortunate enough to have recently participated in a good sex education class, there is probably some information that you've forgotten or never learned. You need to understand fully how your partner functions in order to give him or her maximum pleasure. By reading the recommended books listed at the end of this chapter, you can increase your sexual knowledge. Set a goal of acquiring at least three new pieces of information, whether about anatomical structures, the physiology of orgasm or facts about the effects of aging, illness or stress on sexuality.

Once you're optimally knowledgeable about your partner as a sexual being, you can work on creating a supportive and loving atmosphere for sex. Make it clear to your partner you're not judging his or her performance. Remind him or her that sex is a means of expressing the love you share and not a contest of sexual prowess. By relieving your partner of performance worries, you're enabling him or her to concentrate on the pleasures of sex.

Be careful not to look at sex as an isolated part of your lives. It's often been said that foreplay doesn't begin in the bedroom; everything that happens before a sexual act is still with both of you when you engage in sex. Sex will be loving and romantic only if the rest of your life is also that way.

Spend some time planning ways to add romance outside of the bedroom. Use the following worksheets to record your plans. If you're not currently in a relationship, use the worksheet that begins with "Targeted Area for Adding Romance to

My Life." This will help you develop a more romantic frame of mind and life-style, increasing your readiness for love when it does come along.

If you're in a relationship now, use the worksheet that begins with "Targeted Area for Adding Romance to Our Lives." Completing this worksheet and acting on what you've written will make your shared life more special in nonsexual ways, which should generalize to the sexual arena.

After reading the examples, fill out one of the blank worksheets. Be creative in your plans to add an element of romance to your life.

✳   ✳

TARGETED AREA FOR ADDING ROMANCE TO MY LIFE: Beautifying my apartment.

TECHNIQUES:
1. Buy fresh flowers once a week.
2. Use scented candles.
3. Paint or wallpaper the bedroom.

✳   ✳

✳   ✳

TARGETED AREA FOR ADDING ROMANCE TO MY LIFE: Improving my appearance and self-image.

TECHNIQUES:
1. Wear sexy underwear.
2. Get nails done once a week.
3. Use perfume all the time, not just for special occasions.

✳   ✳

✳   ✳

TARGETED AREA FOR ADDING ROMANCE TO MY LIFE:

_____

TECHNIQUES:

_____

_____

_____

✳   ✳

✳   ✳

TARGETED AREA FOR ADDING ROMANCE TO OUR LIVES: Expressing my love for my partner.

TECHNIQUES:
1. Regularly compliment him or her.
2. Buy a small "I love you" gift once a week.
3. Hug or kiss him a few times each day.

✳   ✳

✳   ✳

TARGETED AREA FOR ADDING ROMANCE TO OUR LIVES: Sharing more special times with each other.

TECHNIQUES:
1. Go out to a nice restaurant for breakfast on Sundays.
2. Plan to spend a quiet night together in front of the fireplace.
3. Take a bubblebath together.

✳   ✳

✳   ✳

TARGETED AREA FOR ADDING ROMANCE TO OUR LIVES:

_____

TECHNIQUES:

_____

_____

_____

✳   ✳

To give your partner maximum pleasure, you really need to concentrate on what you're doing. If you let yourself focus on problems at work or on family arguments, you won't put as much physical or mental energy into pleasuring your partner as you ideally should. It can also be distracting if you try to pleasure each other at the same time. Striving for simultaneous orgasms can be counterproductive in this regard. Neither of you will obtain maximum enjoyment if you're each worrying about the other while receiving stimulation. Taking turns giving and receiving pleasure may give each of you more satisfaction.

Your partner's pleasure is not an obligation to endure. It's a privilege that comes with a loving relationship. Be sure to make the most of this opportunity to express your love in a very tangible and meaningful way.

RECOMMENDED READING

Barbach, Lonnie. *For Yourself: The Fulfillment of Female Sexuality.* New York: Signet, 1975.

Barbach, Lonnie. *For Each Other.* New York: Signet, 1984.

Comfort, Alex. *The Joy of Sex.* New York: Crown, 1987.

Francoeur, Robert T. *Becoming a Sexual Person.* New York: Wiley, 1982.

Freedman, Rita. *BodyLove: Learning to Like Our Looks—and Ourselves.* New York: Harper & Row, 1988.

Heiman, Julia R., and Joseph LoPiccolo. *Becoming Orgasmic: A Sexual and Personal Growth Program for Women.* New York: Prentice-Hall, 1988.

Knopf, Jennifer, and Michael Seiler. *Inhibited Sexual Desire.* New York: Morrow, 1990.

McCarthy, Barry, and Emily McCarthy. *Male Sexual Awareness.* New York: Carroll and Graf, 1988.

McCarthy, Barry, and Emily McCarthy. *Female Sexual Awareness.* New York: Carroll and Graf, 1989.

McCarthy, Barry, and Emily McCarthy. *Couple Sexual Awareness: Sexual Happiness.* New York: Carroll and Graf, 1990.

Zilbergeld, Bernie. *Male Sexuality: A Guide to Sexual Fulfillment.* New York: Bantam Books, 1981.

7

Can You Balance Your Needs with Someone Else's Needs?

If you've ever been involved in a relationship, it will come as no surprise to you that love requires some sacrifices. While there are many rewards to be obtained from loving and being loved, the process also requires putting aside personal needs and desires at times for the sake of the other person. You need to be able to take your partner's feelings into consideration instead of just acting on whatever suits you at the moment.

But you don't have to be a saint or a martyr to make love work. You don't have to give up completely what you want and need in an effort to make the other person happy. It's permissible, and even desirable, to look out for yourself, too. There's no need to focus solely on your partner; it's okay to take care of *you* as well.

Take the following quiz to learn whether you can balance your needs with those of someone else. After you read the profile that describes your functioning in this area, turn to the strategies section to gain some insight into how to achieve this ideal balance.

For each question, choose the one answer that best reflects your way of thinking and behaving.

1. Your partner (past, current or future) is involved in a special project at work and will be home a few hours later than usual. What do you do?
   a. Hold up dinner, making and eating it when he or she comes home.
   b. Have a light snack on your own, instruct your partner to bring home some takeout Chinese and share some of it when he or she gets home.
   c. Go out with a friend and let your partner fend for himself or herself.

2. What's your philosophy and practice concerning giving to charity?
   a. You feel it's important to give something to causes you believe in (and besides, it's a good tax break), but only when you're able to pay your own bills comfortably and have some money left over.
   b. If you were a millionaire, you'd give some money away. But until you reach that point, you've got to look out for yourself. Right now you're your own favorite charity.
   c. Making charitable donations is very important. You feel obligated to give something to charity on a regular basis, regardless of the state of your own finances.

3. Do you usually get gifts you like?
   a. Always. You see to it that everyone in your life knows exactly what to get you.
   b. For the most part. Close friends and relatives have a fairly good understanding of your desires and needs.
   c. Not usually. People never seem to know what you want or like.

4. If you were given a grade for taking care of yourself (e.g., getting enough sleep, taking vitamins, having regular and nutritious meals, getting checkups, exercising and avoiding unsafe sex, drug use or other unhealthy life-style practices), what would it be?
   a. B to C.   b. C− to F.   c. A+ to B+.

5. You're having lunch with a friend at one of your favorite restaurants. She's on a strict diet that prohibits any of the desserts the restaurant is famous for. You find yourself craving the chocolate raspberry mousse. Do you order it?
   a. No. It wouldn't be fair to ask your friend to watch while you savor the mousse.
   b. Only if she agrees to have a cup of coffee or piece of fruit so she won't feel quite so deprived.
   c. Yes. You've been maintaining your ideal weight, so why should you be penalized because your friend has a weight problem?

6. If your town or city did not have mandatory recycling, and the nearest full-service recycling center (for paper, glass, aluminum, platic, etc.) is fifteen miles away, what would you do about recycling?
   a. Although you definitely agree with recycling in theory, it takes more time and space than you can currently devote right now.
   b. You'd go out of your way to recycle everything recyclable, even though it would be a hardship to store the items and make regular trips to the recycling center.
   c. You would save whatever could be recycled most conveniently, such as newspaper if there was a recycling bin for it on your way to work.

7. How hard is it for you to say no to a friend when he or she asks you to do something you'd rather not?
   a. Somewhat difficult. But you manage to say no when you need to.
   b. Pretty easy. You've got to look out for number one, so you don't hesitate to turn down requests you can't or don't want to fulfill.
   c. Very difficult. You seldom turn down any requests.

8. When you were growing up, how important was it for you to please your parents?
   a. Extremely important. You really cared about making them proud of you and devoted yourself to fulfilling their expectations and demands.
   b. Moderately important. You cared about pleasing your parents, but not at your own expense. You weren't willing to sacrifice your needs and wants just to make them happy.

c. Not important. You didn't feel any obligation to try to live up to their expectations and desires for you.

9. A coworker's car is being repaired and he needs a ride to pick it up after work. It's about twenty minutes out of your way and you have a lot of personal errands to do. Will you give him a lift?
   a. Yes. You wouldn't feel right about not helping him out. The errands could be put off till another day.
   b. No. Your time is just too valuable. Your coworker will have to find another way of getting there, such as taking a cab.
   c. If he couldn't find someone else to drive him, you would do it, but you would also run a couple of errands on the way.

10. When you indulge yourself by doing something nice just for yourself, you tend to feel:
   a. Pleased with yourself because you know you deserve it.
   b. A little guilty about what you're doing, but not to the extent you don't do and/or enjoy it.
   c. So guilty about doing it that you usually avoid any indulgences.

11. In any relationship, each person puts in a certain amount of energy, caring and commitment. Fifty-fifty is often considered to be the ideal ratio since both individuals contribute exactly the same amount in the relationship, but this is seldom a reality. Usually one person gives at least a little more, whereas the other gives less. Who usually put(s) more into your past or current relationship?
   a. Too close to call. You and your partner contributed a near-equal amount.
   b. You. Your partner's contributions were (or are) nowhere close to your own.
   c. Your partner. You never put as much into the relationship as the other person.

12. Which of the following do you most agree with?
   a. It's more blessed to give than receive.
   b. Giving and getting are equally fun.
   c. Being at the receiving end is quite enjoyable and isn't anything to be embarrassed or apologetic about.

13. You've agreed to let a friend (who's experiencing some marital problems) stay with you for a while. She has repeatedly told you she doesn't want you to change your life-style while she's there.

You get home from work before she does and usually turn on the TV. What do you do when she gets home?

a. You would watch whatever programs you wanted to, just as if she wasn't there. After all, she did request that you not make any special concessions while she stays with you.

b. Immediately ask her what she prefers to watch. You'd change the channel to her preference or turn it off if she didn't care to watch.

c. You'd finish the program you were watching and then discuss with her what program, if any, to watch next.

14. At an office party, there's a tray of hors d'oeuvres that everyone loves. They're quickly devoured. Only one remains. Would you help yourself to the last one?

   a. Only if other people urged you to take it and you could share it with another person.

   b. Why not? Someone has to take the last one.

   c. Absolutely not. You'd let someone else have it.

15. Are you bothered by "shoulds" and "oughts" (such as "I should have done that differently" or "I ought to do this")?

   a. Occasionally.

   b. Very often.

   c. Seldom, if ever.

16. In terms of going after what you want and fulfilling your needs, the people who know you best would consider you to be:

   a. Passive.

   b. Aggressive.

   c. Assertive.

17. How often do you feel taken advantage of by other people?

   a. Occasionally.

   b. Very infrequently.

   c. Quite often.

18. If you won $150 in a contest sponsored by your employer, what would you do with the money?

   a. Buy yourself something special.

   b. Get a gift for a friend or relative.

   c. Use some of it to take your coworkers out for drinks or to bring a couple of boxes of really good candy to the office and spend the rest on yourself.

19. You would most like people to think of you as:
   a. A very caring and giving person who would give the shirt off your back to someone else if he or she needed it.
   b. A go-getter who doesn't let anything or anyone else stand in your way.
   c. Someone who looks out for number one, but without stepping on anyone else's toes in the process.

20. If you were living with someone who inherited a painting that you disliked intensely, what would you do if he or she wanted to keep it because of the sentimental value?
   a. Refuse to allow it any wall space in your home. (You'd encourage him or her to display it at the office, but you definitely wouldn't live with a piece of art you found ugly.)
   b. Find a place to hang it in your home where you wouldn't have to look at it very often.
   c. Hang it in a prominent spot in your home because it would mean a lot to your partner.

SCORING

Assign yourself points as follows and then add them up.

1.	a- 1	b- 3	c- 5
2.	a- 3	b- 5	c- 1
3.	a- 5	b- 3	c- 1
4.	a- 3	b- 1	c- 5
5.	a- 1	b- 3	c- 5
6.	a- 5	b- 1	c- 3
7.	a- 3	b- 5	c- 1
8.	a- 1	b- 3	c- 5
9.	a- 1	b- 5	c- 3
10.	a- 5	b- 3	c- 1
11.	a- 3	b- 1	c- 5
12.	a- 1	b- 3	c- 5
13.	a- 5	b- 1	c- 3
14.	a- 3	b- 5	c- 1
15.	a- 3	b- 1	c- 5
16.	a- 1	b- 5	c- 3
17.	a- 3	b- 5	c- 1
18.	a- 5	b- 1	c- 3
19.	a- 1	b- 5	c- 3
20.	a- 5	b- 3	c- 1

20 to   52—Other-Oriented
53 to   67—Self-Oriented and Other-Oriented
68 to 100—Self-Oriented

Now turn to the appropriate profile in the next section.

✳ Profiles

Find the profile that corresponds with the score you earned in the quiz section.

OTHER-ORIENTED

You're about as selfless as any human being can be. You truly care about pleasing other people, even at your own expense. It would be completely foreign to your nature to do anything that would hurt anyone else. Even if it was not intentional, you would never want to be the cause of another person's pain, discomfort or even minor inconvenience. You want to tread through life gently, without stepping on anyone's toes. If this requires you to overlook your own needs in the process, so be it. You'd rather make someone else happy than worry about your own well-being.

Your caring knows no limits. Your family, friends, co-workers, neighbors and acquaintances all benefit from your giving nature. But the person who benefits most of all is the one you choose as your partner in love. There's nothing you wouldn't do for this individual. No sacrifice is too big. As far as you're concerned, that's what love is all about.

However, real love is not a one-way street where one person gives and the other takes. In a healthy relationship, both partners look out for each other. But because you're more comfortable catering to the other person's whims and desires than admitting you have any of your own, you're likely to approach love in a very lopsided manner. You want to be on the giving end and expect very little in return. Although you're continually making compromises and sacrifices, it seems like a small price to pay for love.

In reality, it's a tremendous price to pay for finding and keeping love. By focusing solely on other people, you're neglecting the one person who should be the most important in your life: yourself. You may fail to consider your own dreams and may never engage in your individual pursuit of happiness.

You may never find out who you are and what makes you a unique individual, because you're too busy catering to everyone but yourself.

You may be tempted to protest that you *should* be living your life in a way that pleases the person(s) you love. This isn't far from the truth. It's perfectly natural to want the people you care about to be happy and to do whatever is in your power to achieve this goal. But you carry the process too far and you lose your self in the process. You give up what should be important to you and concentrate only on what everyone else wants.

This intense other-orientation can negatively impact upon love. Because you neglect yourself, you don't do much to ensure that you become or remain an interesting person. Your partner will be denied the stimulation that is provided by a person who is actively pursuing his or her own life. Your partner may not see you as an individual in your own right or as an equal. Without this type of respect, your relationship can't realize its fullest potential. Although your partner may at first be flattered by your nonstop attempts to please, he or she may quickly grow tired of it (and you).

Your partner may not be the only one who becomes dissatisfied in the relationship. Remember that your profile began with the sentence "You're about as selfless as any human being can be." This doesn't mean you're completely selfless. Human nature doesn't quite work that way. You can't totally dissociate from yourself and still be a functioning member of society; people who become too detached from themselves are considered to have severe psychiatric problems. At times you can't help but feel resentful about giving more than you get. This resentment is not conducive to love; in fact, it can eventually destroy a relationship.

It's not too late to be on better terms with yourself. You can still care about others, but you can learn to see yourself as a worthwhile individual who is just as deserving of happiness as anyone else. You can learn to please yourself while pleasing others. The strategies section will instruct you in "Becoming More Self-Oriented."

SELF-ORIENTED AND OTHER-ORIENTED

You may never get nominated for sainthood, but no one would ever accuse you of being self-centered or uncaring, either. You've managed to achieve a near-perfect balance between selflessness and selfishness. It isn't always easy, but you try to consider other people's needs as well as your own in everything you do. You're willing to make some sacrifices and compromises when needed. You also expect these things in return from those you care about.

Your dual orientation toward self and others will enable you to handle the give-and-take that's so important in a love relationship. You can be a giving and loving partner who goes out of your way to make your loved one happy. But you'll never lose sight of the fact that *you* deserve to be happy, too. You won't ever find yourself in the unhappy position of always being the giver. Because of your healthy perspective, you'll try to select a partner who will try to reciprocate the love and care you bestow upon him or her. If, along the way, you discover your partner is only interested in his or her own needs and ignores yours, you'll get out of the relationship and try to find someone more like yourself.

Because you're capable of balancing your needs with those of a partner, you can definitely consider yourself ready for love. But it wouldn't hurt for you to read the strategies section for suggestions that will reinforce your functioning in this area. Pay special attention to "Becoming More Self-Oriented" if you scored at the low end of the scale or "Becoming More Other-Oriented" if you found yourself on the scale's higher end.

SELF-ORIENTED

Don't be embarrassed at finding yourself in this category. There is nothing wrong with looking out for yourself. In this world, only those who go after what they want will have a chance of getting it. Instead of pretending that your needs aren't important, you're honest enough to admit that you're not willing to sacrifice your own happiness just to please someone else. It's not that you don't think other people deserve to be happy; it's simply that you're your number one priority.

This is a healthy attitude for the most part. While it may not always be appreciated by the people you interact with, it does ensure that they won't be in a position to take advantage of you. Your friends, family, coworkers and acquaintances probably respect your unwavering determination to get what you want out of life. They may occasionally begrudge you your successes and your aggressiveness in obtaining them, but they'll usually be careful not to stand in your way as you pursue what's important to you.

But there is one area of your life where your self-orientation can be dysfunctional. Love requires the ability to balance your needs with those of your partner. You can't be so concerned with your own desires that you ignore his or hers. In a caring relationship, both partners need to be working together to ensure their mutual satisfaction. If each of you wants only to fulfull your individual goals, you won't have much of a partnership. All you'll have is one endless competition where there's inevitably one winner and one loser.

It would be ridiculous to imply that love is only meaningful when the needs of both partners are equally met at all times. Any time two people are involved in a relationship, they bring their own wants, concerns and personalities with them. No matter how many similarities a couple may share, there are still bound to be some issues and perspectives that can't be shared completely. No two people can be in perfect accord all the time.

But it's crucial for both partners to make some attempt to acknowledge each other's needs and to work together in accommodating those individual needs within the framework of a relationship. Unfortunately, this is where you're frequently not up to the task. Your self-involvement prevents you from taking the time and effort to examine what your partner wants. If he or she is not very assertive or vocal about his or her own requirements for happiness, you may never know what they are. This lack of knowledge results in a lack of emotional intimacy; you have no idea of your partner's dreams, ambitions and preferences because you're too busy pursuing your own.

Another concern is your unwillingness to compromise. Even if you suspect or actually know what pleases your partner, it can be difficult for you to provide it for him or her, especially if it conflicts with what you want. Because it's so important to have things your way, you're often not amenable to making concessions for the sake of your partner and the relationship. Instead of seeing compromise as a win-win situation, you feel that it means you failed because you didn't get everything you wanted.

Obviously, this can create some problems in loving and in being loved. Your partner may resent what he or she considers to be your selfishness and may feel that you really don't care. You'll be depriving yourself of the satisfaction that comes from fully sharing and giving of yourself. Your relationship will lack the trust, compassion and intimacy that makes true love so special.

Your orientation toward self works well in business and athletics. Both provide an arena to pursue singlemindedly what you want, even if it hurts someone else in the process. But it's imperative for you to become more oriented toward others (specifically, your "significant other") if you also want to succeed in love. To learn how to do this, read "Becoming More Other-Oriented" in the strategies section.

✳ Strategies for Balancing Your Needs with Those of Someone Else

Read the appropriate section to learn how to achieve mutual satisfaction by successfully balancing both your own and your partner's wants and needs.

BECOMING MORE SELF-ORIENTED

As a child, you were probably taught to think of others before yourself. At home, school and church, it was drilled into your head that selflessness was far more preferable than even the slightest hint of selfishness. You took these teachings seriously, and to this day you are still acting on them. So it won't be easy to shift your focus to yourself. But to become more ready for love, you must stop minimizing your own wants and needs and start trying to please yourself.

The process of becoming more self-oriented will undoubtedly cause intense feelings of guilt to surface. You'll feel at first that you are doing something very wrong when you concentrate on being good to yourself. These initial feelings of shame and embarrassment should pass as you become more comfortable with recognizing that you deserve happiness just as much as anyone else. When you work through the guilt and come to terms with your responsibility to ensure your own satisfaction in life and love, you'll be well on the road to becoming self-oriented in a healthy way.

To help you leave behind the feelings of guilt that may run rampant as you embark on your new approach, you must abandon all the "shoulds" and "oughts" you're convinced you must live under. While there may be some rules and obligations associated with your job, there don't have to be many in the private parts of your life. You may feel inundated by a never-ending series of shoulds in your own relationship(s), but that feeling is of your own making. Even if your partner tells you what you should be doing, it's ultimately *your* decision whether or not to incorporate this into your consciousness. You can control what you embrace as your obligations to other people as well as to yourself, so you need never feel overwhelmed.

On a piece of paper, write down all the "shoulds" and "oughts" you subscribe to. Concentrate on those things that relate to what you feel a good love partner should be or do. Base your answers on what you experienced in past relationships and in a current one, if applicable. It can also be helpful to include the shoulds associated with the roles you play in your other relationships, such as daughter, sister, mother and friend. Don't worry about grammar or spelling; just jot down as many things as you think you should be doing or feeling because other people expect it or because it's the right thing to do. The following examples are only a few possibilities:

- I should . . . *be willing to do whatever it takes to make my partner happy.*
- I ought . . . *to be having sex more.*

- I should . . . *try to look perfect all the time.*
- I should not . . . *be concerned about myself when I have other people to worry about.*
- I ought . . . *to throw more parties for my friends.*
- I should . . . *visit my mother twice a week.*
- I should not . . . *express any concerns about our financial situation since it upsets my partner.*
- I should . . . *act as if I'm not very interested when I meet someone new so I don't appear desperate.*

Once you write down all your shoulds and oughts, you can study them to see whether any are really valid. Chances are, if you really consider what you've written, you'll decide only a few of them are really necessary. Your intentions may have been good when you formulated them, but the end result is that you've convinced yourself to do some things you may not want to do simply out of fear, guilt, shame or misinformation. Even if you do or don't do certain things because you're afraid of the interpersonal consequences (what other people will think, say or do), you'll still be faced with some disturbing consequences of a personal nature: your unhappiness with doing what you don't want to do or not doing what you want to.

Now rip up your list and throw it away. This act will symbolize that you're no longer retaining all those shoulds in your mind. By discarding all the obligations imposed by yourself and others, you'll find yourself free to pick and choose voluntarily what's right for you. You can decide rationally how you want to play out your relationships and live your life.

When you no longer are tormented by your shoulds, you'll find it easier to say no to other people when they make unacceptable demands. If you still have difficulty turning down requests and ignoring unreasonable expectations, consider reading books or taking a workshop that will instruct you on how to become more assertive.

As you work on increasing your assertiveness, you'll also want to focus on telling people what you need. It's both unfair and unrealistic to expect even the person(s) closest to you to know exactly what it is you want without your telling them. They may have many terrific qualities, but mind reading is not likely to be one of them. Become more vocal about what you'd like from other people. Think of someone you care about and who cares about you. This person probably falls short of providing you with something you'd like, but you've never informed him or her of what that is. For example, maybe you'd like him or her to listen more instead of monopolizing the conversation about his or her own concerns. Perhaps you have a friend who forgets your birthday and you've secretly been fuming about it every year. Decide what it is you haven't been getting but would like to get from this person. Then ask for it! After studying the example, commit yourself to taking action by filling out the following worksheet and then implement it as soon as possible. Once you achieve some success and see it's not so difficult to speak up and make requests of someone else, you can begin to do it on a regular basis with a variety of people in your life.

❋   ❋

WHO: My mother.

WHAT I HAVEN'T BEEN GETTING FROM HER: Any praise or compliments about my achievements and my accomplishments.

WHAT I'LL REQUEST FROM HER: That she occasionally let me know that she's proud of me.

❋   ❋

❋   ❋

WHO: _____

WHAT I HAVEN'T BEEN GETTING FROM HIM OR HER:

_____

_____

WHAT I'LL REQUEST FROM HIM OR HER: _____

_____

_____

❋   ❋

Taking care of yourself is one of the most important aspects of a healthy self-orientation. If you don't feel good physically and psychologically, you won't be able fully to love and be loved. Resolve now to take some simple but meaningful steps to improve your well-being. Read the examples on the illustrated worksheet, then fill out your own specific plans for maximizing your health.

✳   ✳

To ensure that I feel and look as good as I possibly can, I will immediately begin to make these changes.

_____ DIET: Reduce my consumption of meat, ice cream and other high-cholesterol items.

_____ EXERCISE: Work out with weights twice a week and do aerobics three times weekly.

_____ SLEEP: Get eight hours a night and buy a better mattress.

_____ SUBSTANCE USE (alcohol, drugs, cigarettes, caffeine): Reduce caffeine consumption by limiting myself to two cups of coffee a day and drinking soft drinks without caffeine.

_____ SAFETY: Always wear my seatbelt. Take a self-defense course.

_____ PREVENTIVE MEDICAL CARE: Go to the dentist twice a year. Get my cholesterol checked once a year.

✳   ✳

✳   ✳

To ensure that I feel and look as good as I possibly can, I will immediately begin to make these changes.

_____ DIET: _____

_____

_____

_____ EXERCISE: _____

_____

_____

_____ SLEEP: _____

_____

_____

_____ SUBSTANCE USE (alcohol, drugs, cigarettes, caffeine): _____

_____

_____

_____ SAFETY: _____

_____

_____

_____ PREVENTIVE MEDICAL CARE: _____

_____

_____

✳   ✳

Hardest of all for someone who puts others first is any self-indulgence. You probably find it difficult, if not impossible, to be good to yourself. As long as there's anyone else you can do something for, you'll ignore your own desires and concentrate on making the other person happy. But the fact that you're reading this indicates an awareness that you can't continue to live the rest of your life this way. You must start looking out for yourself if you want to give and receive love in a relationship that will work for both you and your partner.

The next exercise will force you to designate a daily time and activity in which you think only of yourself. All thoughts about other people and what you could be doing for them need to be banished from your mind. Although the time and activity can vary from day to day, the one constant must be that you indulge yourself every day, even if only in a small way and for only a few minutes. Make this as much a daily ritual as showering or brushing your teeth. After studying the example that follows, fill out your own worksheet to reflect a week of these plans. Get in the habit of mapping out such plans every week (at least mentally if not physically) and make sure you follow them without missing a day.

✳   ✳

DAILY SELF-INDULGENCE SCHEDULE

DAY: Sunday
TIME: 10 A.M. to 10:30 A.M.
ACTIVITY: Doing the *New York Times* crossword puzzle

DAY: Monday
TIME: All night long
ACTIVITY: Listening to music (and taking the phone off the hook so I'm not disturbed)

DAY: Tuesday
TIME: 8:15 P.M. to 8:35 P.M.
ACTIVITY: Making a long-distance call to a friend who lives abroad

DAY: Wednesday
TIME: 5:30 P.M. to 5:45 P.M.
ACTIVITY: Stopping off at a floral shop on my way home from work and buying some flowers for myself

DAY: Thursday
TIME: Breakfast
ACTIVITY: Making French toast for myself

DAY: Friday
TIME: Lunch hour
ACTIVITY: Shopping for new cosmetics

DAY: Saturday
TIME: 1 P.M. to 2 P.M.
ACTIVITY: Getting my nails done

✳   ✳

✻   ✻

D A I L Y   S E L F - I N D U L G E N C E   S C H E D U L E

DAY: Sunday

TIME: _____

ACTIVITY: _____

DAY: Monday

TIME: _____

ACTIVITY: _____

DAY: Tuesday

TIME: _____

ACTIVITY: _____

DAY: Wednesday

TIME: _____

ACTIVITY: _____

DAY: Thursday

TIME: _____

ACTIVITY: _____

DAY: Friday

TIME: _____

ACTIVITY: _____

DAY: Saturday

TIME: _____

ACTIVITY: _____

✻   ✻

As you embark on your quest to become more self-oriented, try not to worry about becoming so selfish that you neglect the needs of the person(s) you love. You don't have it in your nature to become an uncaring or thoughtless person. You're simply striving to become self-centered in the best sense of the word—knowing what you want and realizing that you deserve it. The contentment that will follow from pursuing this philosophy will make you a more loving and lovable person. You'll truly be ready for love.

BECOMING MORE OTHER-ORIENTED

Looking out for yourself is something you do well, and that's to your advantage. It's a critical ability for loving and for being loved. This ability needs to remain intact throughout your life. You don't want to diminish it in any way. But it's also important that you expand your orientation to include other people as well as yourself. You can continue to be self-oriented, but you need to become other-oriented, too. If you really want to be ready for love, you must possess this dual orientation.

Because you already have a strong self-focus, what remains is to acquire more of a focus on other people in general, and your future or present partner in particular. Your new approach should concentrate on putting sufficient time and energy into considering the impact your actions have on others. Instead of thinking only of yourself, you need to remember that you don't live in a vacuum. Almost everything you say or do can affect the people around you, so you must take care to conduct yourself in a way that won't hurt anyone else.

Your active self-orientation may blind you to those occasions when you cause pain, discomfort or unhappiness to others. You probably aren't aware of these instances, but your family, friends and acquaintances undoubtedly are. Enlist their help in alerting you to the ways in which you ignored their needs in your zealous quest to satisfy your own. Ask them to tell you when you step on their toes. You might want to compile a list to remind you of what you've done in the past or present to hurt others. It won't be pleasant to learn how you may have ignored other people's needs and possibly even abused their rights, but it will be eye-opening. Once you're faced with the realization that you have the power to hurt the people you care about, you can work on curbing that power so further violations are minimized.

But you can't stop there; it's not enough merely to avoid hurting someone else. You need to take an active role in helping to satisfy the needs and wants of the person(s) you love. Really to live love and not just give lip service to it, you must go out of your way to promote the other person's happiness. The problem is you may not have even the slightest idea of what anyone else wants because you've been focusing exclusively on what *you* want. Turn the tables now and do some investigative work to find out what the person you care about (a partner if you have one, otherwise a good friend or relative) wants from life, from love, and from you. Ask him or her to reveal those desires and listen well. Don't attempt to interject your own thoughts on the subject. Remember this isn't about you; it's about the other person. (It can be difficult to write down this response since it may be vague, complicated or very lengthy, so you don't need to attempt to record it on a worksheet. Do make sure, however, that you have a clear understanding of what you're told.)

You can consider yourself to be more other-oriented as you increase your awareness of what's important to other people. But you're still not all the way there. While knowledge is one thing, action is quite another. Now that you're cognizant of the needs of others, you must resolve to help fulfill some of them. You're not expected to devote yourself exclusively to this project; it's still important that you live your life to suit yourself for the most part. But if you want love in your life, you can't continue to live in a way that only focuses on your needs and disregards those of anyone else.

Each day you must set aside some time and energy to do something for someone else. Make sure it will be meaningful and enjoyable for this person. Don't impose your own values and needs on your plans; remember that the focus is on the other person. For example, you won't bake a fudge walnut torte for a friend who's allergic to chocolate, even if you're a confirmed chocoholic! Read the illustrated worksheet, then fill

✳   ✳

DAILY PLANS FOR DOING SOMETHING FOR SOMEONE ELSE

DAY: Sunday
Time: 2 P.M. to 3 P.M.
TARGETED PERSON(S): Mrs. Smith (neighbor)
ACTIVITY: Check in on her and see how she's doing since returning from the hospital; offer to do some chores for her, such as shopping or walking the dog

DAY: Monday
TIME: Lunchtime
TARGETED PERSON(S): Tim (coworker)
ACTIVITY: Bring him back some lunch since he's too busy to get away himself

DAY: Tuesday
TIME: About 8 P.M. while I pay some bills
TARGETED PERSON(S): Abused children
ACTIVITY: Write a check for the local children's shelter

DAY: Wednesday
TIME: 7 P.M. to 10 P.M.
TARGETED PERSON(S): Mary (close friend)
ACTIVITY: Bring over a casserole for dinner and provide a sympathetic ear so she can vent her feelings about losing her job

DAY: Thursday
TIME: 7 P.M. to 8:30 P.M.
TARGETED PERSON(S): Allen (nephew)
ACTIVITY: Watch him in his school play

DAY: Friday
TIME: Sometime during work
TARGETED PERSON(S): Sonia (coworker)
ACTIVITY: Give her a "cheer-up" card that reminds her that things will get better and that people care about her, especially since she's experiencing some family problems right now

DAY: Saturday
TIME: 2 to ?
TARGETED PERSON(S): Peter (friend)
ACTIVITY: Help him study for his law school test, then suggest we do something fun in the evening to help him get his mind off the upcoming exam

✳   ✳

out the blank one on your own. Be sure to make plans for *every* day of the week.

---

*   *

DAILY PLANS FOR DOING SOMETHING FOR SOMEONE ELSE

DAY: Sunday

TIME: _____

TARGETED PERSON(S): _____

ACTIVITY: _____

_____

_____

DAY: Monday

TIME: _____

TARGETED PERSON(S): _____

ACTIVITY: _____

_____

_____

DAY: Tuesday

TIME: _____

TARGETED PERSON(S): _____

ACTIVITY: _____

_____

_____

DAY: Wednesday

TIME: _____

TARGETED PERSON(S): _____

ACTIVITY: _____

_____

_____

DAY: Thursday

TIME: _____

TARGETED PERSON(S): _____

ACTIVITY: _____

_____

_____

DAY: Friday

TIME: _____

TARGETED PERSON(S): _____

ACTIVITY: _____

_____

_____

DAY: Saturday

TIME: _____

TARGETED PERSON(S): _____

ACTIVITY: _____

_____

_____

✳   ✳

Your goal is to do something on a daily basis that fulfills the needs of someone else. You'll discover that caring for others in a tangible way has just as many rewards as caring for yourself. By developing expertise in balancing your needs with the needs of others, you'll ensure that you're optimally ready for love.

RECOMMENDED READING

Bach, George R., and Laura Torber. *A Time for Caring.* New York: Delacorte, 1982.

Blaker, Karen. *Born to Please.* New York: St. Martin's Press, 1988.

Leman, Kevin. *The Pleasers: Women Who Can't Say No and the Men Who Control Them.* New York: Dell, 1987.

Paul, Jordan, and Margaret Paul. *Do I Have to Give Up Me to Be Loved By You?* Minneapolis: CompCare, 1983.

Seabury, David. *The Art of Selfishness.* New York: Pocket Books, 1981.

8

Are Your Communication Skills Sufficient for Love?

In romance novels, the hero and heroine don't have to speak to communicate their thoughts and feelings. They're so in touch with each other, they intuitively know what's in their loved one's heart and mind. A fleeting glance or touch can be all they need to express themselves on the most intimate of levels.

But in real life and love, communication isn't quite so effortless. It can be extremely difficult for two people really to connect and communicate, regardless of how much they love each other. Busy lives may limit opportunities to share thoughts and feelings on anything more than a superficial level. A lack of knowledge and skill can also contribute to less than optimal communication in a love relationship.

Being able to communicate is an essential prerequisite for love. Find out whether your communication skills are adequate for a love relationship by taking the quiz and reading your profile. Suggestions are offered in the strategies section for improving your ability to communicate.

✳ # QUIZ ✳

Choose one answer for each question.

1. You and a friend agree to get together for dinner. When your friend asks what restaurant you'd like to go to, your typical response is to:
   a. Hesitate and say you don't know.
   b. Ask what type of food your friend is in the mood for.
   c. Name the restaurant that most appeals to you at the moment.

2. Your friends would describe you as:
   a. Talkative.
   b. Somewhere between talkative and quiet, or talkative at some times and quiet at others.
   c. Quiet.

3. What would you most like in terms of communicating with your partner?
   a. A partner who really knows how to listen.
   b. Not having to spell out everything, but for him or her to know intuitively what you're thinking and feeling.
   c. A give-and-take style, where we both talk with (not at) each other.

4. How many of your coworkers know the details of your personal life (e.g., problems in your relationship)?
   a. A few.
   b. Most or all.
   c. None.

5. What are your thoughts on you and your partner having secrets from each other?
   a. Even in the closest of relationships, people deserve a great deal of privacy.
   b. It's unacceptable, because two people who love each other should share everything and not have any secrets.
   c. As long as the really important things that impact both of you are shared, it's okay not to tell each other absolutely everything.

6. Your policy on openness and honesty is:
   a. To be as candid as possible without hurting anyone else's feelings.
   b. Not to reveal more than you have to because you never know when it will come back to haunt you.
   c. To strive to be forthright and truthful at all times, no matter what.

7. How easy is it for you to admit when you're wrong and apologize?
   a. Extremely easy.
   b. Not easy, but you can usually manage it.
   c. Extremely difficult.

8. Your usual listening style is:
   a. Quiet and passive, so the other person won't be distracted when talking.
   b. Fully participatory, often interjecting your own thoughts and feelings.
   c. Attentive, occasionally nodding your head or making listening noises such as "uh-huh."

9. How well do you read other people's body language?
   a. Not very well. It's too inexact a science to be credible and you don't know much about it, so you concentrate exclusively on verbal communication.
   b. Fairly well, depending on the person. You find it advantageous to consider both verbal and nonverbal communication in your dealings with others.
   c. Extremely well. In fact, you feel a person's posture and gestures are much more important than his or her words.

10. If you were annoyed at your partner for repeatedly leaving the bathroom sink dirty, what would you be most likely to say?
    a. "Why don't you ever pick up after yourself? How could you be so lazy and thoughtless?"
    b. "Try to be more considerate."
    c. "When the sink is left like that, I feel like I have no choice but to clean it myself since I can't stand the mess, but I feel that I'm being used as a free maid service."

11. When you argue, you most want to:
    a. Resolve the issue as much as it can be resolved.

  b. End it as soon as possible and keep the damage to a minimum.
  c. Let your feelings be known and win the argument.

12. On a blind date, you would tend to:
  a. Let your date take the lead in setting the conversational pace and agenda. You would focus on answering questions but would not volunteer much information about yourself.
  b. Try to ascertain what topics are of mutual interest and stick to those. You would ask questions as well as volunteer an equal amount of personal information.
  c. Assume the conversational lead. You feel this would prevent your date from feeling interrogated by too many questions and would also enable him or her to quickly learn all about you.

13. A friend changes her hair color, becoming a platinum blonde. She asks you what you honestly think. Do you tell her the truth and let her know how artificial and unflattering it is?
  a. Not in so many words. You would say you have some trouble adjusting to change, so you're a little more comfortable with the previous brunette color.
  b. Yes. As a friend, you have the obligation to let her know how awful it looks.
  c. No. It's a done deed, so why make her feel bad about it? You would tell her that it looks great.

14. In a love relationship, how would you let your partner know that he or she was loved?
  a. You would make sure you frequently told your partner that you loved him or her.
  b. You would try to tell your partner every so often you loved him or her, as well as showing your love through nonverbal means.
  c. You would let your actions speak for themselves. Your commitment and caring would be obvious to your partner, so words wouldn't be needed.

15. Which of the following seminars would you like to attend?
  a. How to Be a Better Conversationalist.
  b. How to Say More in Less Time.
  c. Sharpening Your Communication Skills.

16. Should two people who really love each other exchange angry words?

a. No. A love relationship needs to avoid negativity.

b. Occasionally. It's sometimes okay and even necessary to argue about certain issues, provided it's done fairly.

c. Yes. It's important they both know exactly what the other is thinking and feeling, even when it creates some friction.

17. Which do you tend to regret the most?

a. Things you didn't say.

b. Things you said that didn't quite come out the way you would have liked.

c. Things you said you shouldn't have.

SCORING

Add up your points as follows.

1. a- 1	b- 3	c- 5
2. a- 5	b- 3	c- 1
3. a- 5	b- 1	c- 3
4. a- 3	b- 5	c- 1
5. a- 1	b- 5	c- 3
6. a- 3	b- 1	c- 5
7. a- 5	b- 3	c- 1
8. a- 1	b- 5	c- 3
9. a- 1	b- 3	c- 5
10. a- 5	b- 1	c- 3
11. a- 3	b- 1	c- 5
12. a- 3	b- 5	c- 1
13. a- 1	b- 3	c- 5
14. a- 5	b- 3	c- 1
15. a- 1	b- 5	c- 3
16. a- 1	b- 3	c- 5
17. a- 1	b- 5	c- 3

Find the range in which your score falls, then turn to the corresponding profile.

17–37—Minimally Communicative
38–64—Communicative
65–85—Overly Communicative

✳ Profiles

Find the profile that corresponds to the score you earned in the quiz section.

MINIMALLY COMMUNICATIVE

Although your communication skills may be limited in scope and intensity, this doesn't reflect a lack of thoughts and feelings. To the contrary, your emotional and intellectual makeup is as deep and complex as anyone else's. But whereas other people can easily share what they're thinking and feeling, you tend to keep it to yourself.

The cause of your reticence is not important. You may be quiet because your parents encouraged you to "be seen and not heard" or because you lack confidence in yourself and can't believe you have anything of worth to say. It may simply be your nature to keep things bottled inside you rather than to express them. Whatever the reason, the end result is the same: limited communication.

This is not to imply that you lack verbal ability. You may have an excellent command of language and be extremely articulate. Being minimally communicative doesn't automatically mean you never say a word. It's quite likely you can carry your share of the conversation or make yourself understood. Casual communication may not present any problems at all.

But an ability to communicate with a stranger or a business acquaintance is one thing. Communicating with a partner in a love relationship is worlds apart from objectively relaying factual information or making small talk. An intimate relationship demands intimate communication. If you're going to be involved with someone on more than a superficial level, you need to be able to share what's in your heart and on your mind.

The one aspect of communication that you probably excel at is listening. Chances are you're an expert listener who allows other people to express themselves. Because you're not prone to interrupting or to listening with only half an ear while you think about what you're going to say next, you may be much better at listening than more talkative individuals. Listening is definitely an essential part of communication in any relationship. The person you love should consider himself or herself fortunate in having a partner who knows how to listen so well.

While listening is an admirable and essential skill, it is only one part of the total communication you need in love. A one-sided arrangement where your partner divulges his or her innermost thoughts and feelings without any reciprocation on your part deprives both of you of communication in its fullest sense. To experience the ultimate in communication in a love relationship, you must learn to open up and express yourself.

You may not have been born with the gift of gab, but that's not a problem. With a little work, you can acquire the ability to share the real you with your partner. The strategies section will instruct you on "Developing Your Communication Skills."

COMMUNICATIVE

You may not always know exactly the right thing to say, and sometimes you might not listen as well as you should, but you generally are skilled at communication. You appear to understand that communication is a give-and-take process requiring considerable thought and effort. Although it can be risky and stressful to reveal your thoughts and feelings, you're willing to do so because you want to share yourself with the people you care about. But because you moderate your communication, you're not given to excesses. You avoid going overboard and refrain from divulging everything you think and feel. You know what you don't say can be just as important as what you do say. The truth is something you strive to tell, but not at the expense of another person's feelings.

The balanced approach you bring to communication is reflected in your equal abilities to listen *and* to express yourself. Whereas other people tend to be either talkers or listeners, you manage to do both well. This dual ability works to your benefit in any relationship, but it is especially beneficial to love. Assuming that your partner has equivalent communication skills, the two of you should enjoy an atmosphere where you feel free to reveal yourselves without fear of ridicule, misunderstanding or rejection. This level of intimate communication helps love to develop and grow. No matter what problems are encountered in your relationship(s), there will always be a fighting chance of keeping love alive when you're able to communicate with each other.

Although you're in an enviable position in terms of your communication skills, you want to be sure to maintain and enhance them. You may gain some insight into how to do this by reading the information in the strategies section. If your score was on the lower end of the range, you can concentrate on "Developing Your Communication Skills." If it was on the higher end, your focus should be on "Refining Your Communication Skills." A score exactly in the middle calls for congratulations, but read both subsections anyway, to ensure that your communication skills remain at this optimal level.

OVERLY COMMUNICATIVE

Obviously communication is a desirable commodity, especially in a love relationship. You may wonder, then, how it's possible for you to have fallen into the overly communicative category. If love needs adequate communication to develop and grow, can there ever be too much of it?

In a word, yes. There *can* be too much of a good thing. Just as we require food and water to stay alive, communication is an essential nutrient for the vitality of a relationship. But an excess of any of these (food, water or communication) can cause significant problems and be extremely unhealthy.

In some ways, your tendency to hypercommunicate can be used to your advantage. You certainly won't hesitate to make your voice heard. Whereas other people are shy about speaking up, you have no qualms about doing so. Whenever you're around, people won't have to endure any uncomfortable silences. You can always be counted on to keep the conversation going.

But communication in a love relationship requires more than just the ability to chatter away. Both partners need to be able to express their thoughts and feelings, but the person you love may never get a chance to interject anything of his or her own because of your loquaciousness. Your partner may become frustrated at the lack of opportunity to share his or her concerns with you. In turn, he or she may stop listening to you because there's such an overload of verbalization running everything together that nothing stands out as being really important.

Still another problem is that you probably don't monitor what you say. You may blurt out things without thinking and then find out the other person was hurt by them. You may be excessively honest, refusing ever to resort to any white lies, and neglect to exercise enough tact to avoid causing pain to the other person. Arguments may get completely out of hand if you persist in saying whatever is on your mind.

Your glibness may cause your partner not to take you seriously at times. It's so easy for you to say anything that you wind up losing some credibility. Whether you're apologizing or telling your partner that you love him or her, the words may not be perceived as being real or meaningful because they may roll off your tongue without any thought or action to back them up.

You don't need to give up your communicativeness totally and take a vow of silence, to become more ready for love. All you have to do is modify your communication style so it works for, not against, love. Learn about "Refining Your Communication Skills" in the strategies section.

✴   Strategies for Improving Your Communication Skills

Adequate communication is crucial for any love relationship. Fortunately, skills in listening and talking can be acquired fairly easily. This section will show you how.

DEVELOPING YOUR COMMUNICATION SKILLS

You've already developed expertise in listening, so you don't need to worry about that particular communication skill. You can concentrate instead on improving your ability to express yourself. Accomplishing this isn't nearly as difficult as it might sound. You're not expected to change overnight into a nonstop talker; in fact, you don't ever need to become something you're not. You only need to have the desire to share yourself with the person(s) you most care about and then develop the ability to express your thoughts and feelings without holding back.

There's no objective means for measuring success in self-expression. You won't be given grades for your performance, nor will you be able to use a handy checklist for critiquing yourself. What and how you communicate is totally up to you. You'll know you're successful at it when it feels right for you. When you're comfortable with letting your partner know who you really are and what's in your mind and heart, you can consider yourself to be adequately communicative.

Begin by breaking down the barriers to your opening up and revealing your innermost self. If you've never developed this ability due to a lack of opportunity (e.g., not having anyone who was interested enough to want this from you), find or make some opportunities and *practice*. If you lack self-confidence and don't believe you have anything of value or interest to say to anyone (even the person who loves you), work on developing a better self-image. Read self-help books, join a support group, or seek counseling so you can learn to like and respect yourself more.

One of the first ways you can start to reveal your thoughts and feelings is by avoiding "I don't know" or "I'm not sure" responses. Instead of hesitating and hedging when you're asked a question about what you want or what you think, you need to take a stand. If it's something really major, it's natural and prudent for you to take some time to respond while you sort out your feelings. But with relatively inconsequential matters, such as what videotape to rent, try to make an immediate response.

The worksheet below will require you to keep a minidiary of your progress in giving specific answers to your friends, coworkers, neighbors or partner if you're currently involved in a relationship. Write in the date, the actual question, your response, the reason(s) behind the response, and a rating (" + " if the response was specific and " − " if it was noncommittal). Read the examples and then use the blank worksheet to track your progress. You'll need to write down each instance where

you gave an answer that revealed your true thoughts and
feelings, as well as those times when you did not. Keep up
your recording until there are at least six instances in a row
where you received plusses. This will indicate that you're
establishing a pattern of self-disclosure.

✻   ✻

DATE: February 15th

QUESTION: My sister asked me what movie I'd like to see.

RESPONSE/NONRESPONSE: "The new Mel Gibson movie."

REASON(S) BEHIND THE RESPONSE/NONRESPONSE: Because that's
what I felt like seeing!

RATING: +

DATE: February 19th

QUESTION: A coworker asked me what I thought of the new health
insurance my company is providing.

RESPONSE/NONRESPONSE: "I'm not sure."

REASON(S) BEHIND RESPONSE/NONRESPONSE: Not wanting to give an
answer that might be contrary to the coworker's opinion.

RATING: −

✻   ✻

```
✳                                                    ✳
  DATE: _____

  QUESTION: _____

  _____

  RESPONSE/NONRESPONSE: _____

  _____

  REASON(S) BEHIND RESPONSE/NONRESPONSE: _____

  _____

  RATING: _____
✳                                                    ✳
```

You can then proceed to the next level of self-expression. At this stage, you don't need to wait for an actual question before you offer your opinion or reveal how you feel. Whenever the opportunity presents itself for you to voice your perceptions or needs, do so. You don't need to wait for an invitation. The worksheet you'll use is almost identical to the first one you filled out, but this time you'll be writing down a situation rather than a question. Study the example, then write in your own experiences as they occur. Again, keep recording until you establish six successive occasions where you were assertive about revealing your thoughts and emotions.

```
✳                                                    ✳
  DATE: March 12th

  SITUATION: My partner arranged a dinner date for us without checking
  with me first.

  RESPONSE/NONRESPONSE: I didn't say anything when he told me
  about it, even though I wasn't in the mood to socialize tonight.

  REASON(S) BEHIND RESPONSE/NONRESPONSE: Trying to make the
  best of a bad situation. I didn't want us both to be in a bad mood.

  RATING: −
✳                                                    ✳
```

✳

DATE: March 13th

SITUATION: A coworker was telling ethnic jokes that I found offensive.

RESPONSE/NONRESPONSE: I told him that these jokes made me uncomfortable and that I would prefer him to tell jokes that didn't poke fun at certain racial, religious or ethnic groups.

REASON(S) BEHIND RESPONSE/NONRESPONSE: In addition to disliking ethnic jokes on general principles, these jokes were inappropriate for the workplace and I was unwilling to keep quiet while he continued to offend me as well as other coworkers.

RATING: +

✳   ✳

✳

DATE: _____

SITUATION: _____

_____

RESPONSE/NONRESPONSE: _____

_____

REASON(S) BEHIND RESPONSE/NONRESPONSE: _____

_____

RATING: _____

✳   ✳

After achieving some success in expressing yourself when opportunities present themselves, you can then begin to target specific circumstances when you'll speak up. Perhaps you'll want to voice a criticism or complaint. Maybe you'll need to give a long overdue compliment. It may be an observation or opinion. It could involve taking a risk, such as declaring your love for another person before you're sure of how he or she feels about you. Whatever it is you want to communicate, decide ahead of time when, where and how you'll say what you need to. Write down the general trend of your intended communication and don't throw the paper away until you accomplish your mission!

You'll eventually need to break down the final barrier. You probably know exactly what you find to be the hardest thing to talk about, but if not, you can do some introspective searching to discover this "hot" topic. Sex, politics, traumatic childhood experiences, past relationships or money are just a few of the possibilities. Only you can decide what presents the most difficulty for you. Don't rush into this last step—be sure you're ready to tackle an emotionally charged issue. When it feels comfortable, you can begin to articulate some of your thoughts and feelings about the subject to your partner or a trusted friend.

Reducing your reluctance to reveal yourself won't happen overnight. It's a process that will cause you some discomfort at first. But gradually, you'll find that your communication comfort zone is expanding. Both you and your partner (actual or future) will benefit from the enhanced communication skills you worked so hard on developing.

REFINING YOUR COMMUNICATION SKILLS

You don't need to learn to communicate more; you just need to communicate *better.* You already have the basic foundation for optimal talking and listening. All that remains to be done is to refine those skills so they can be used to maximum benefit.

Listening is a good place to start. While your conversational skills are admirable, it's unlikely that any partner would want to hear endless monologues. To be effective, communication must be a two-way street where both partners are able to express themselves. But your partner will never be able to do this if you persist in monopolizing the conversation, or if you listen with only half an ear.

You may tend to interrupt frequently when others are

talking. It's important for you to be aware of this behavior and to work toward decreasing instances when it occurs. Interrupting may occur so naturally that you don't even know you're doing it, so ask a close friend to call it to your attention every time it happens.

With a little conscious effort, you should find that you seldom interrupt any more. But it takes more than this to be a good listener. If you're thinking of something else or merely biding your time until it's your turn to speak, you won't be devoting enough energy to really hearing what the other person is saying. Learn to become an active listener, fully concentrating on the speaker's words and nonverbal expression. You also need to put considerable effort into understanding what is being expressed. But avoid the temptation to play amateur psychologist or mind reader. Do not attempt to tell someone else what he or she is thinking or feeling. Instead, mirror back what you heard the other person say and check to see whether you heard correctly.

Once you improve your listening skills, you can work on refining your ability to express yourself. There are four major communication errors you may be making. You'll be well on your way to more successful communication just by being able to recognize the mistakes you make.

A hypercommunicative individual like yourself is often prone to communicating without integrity. Talking comes so easily to you that the words pour out without much thought. The problem is that quantity isn't synonymous with quality. You may say things that you don't really mean. When this is the case, everything you say can become suspect. People won't know what is true and heartfelt and what isn't. If you make promises that aren't kept, their value quickly decreases. Your promises become nothing more than empty words that no one trusts.

But this is not to say you have to tell the truth, the whole truth and nothing but in every communication. You need to monitor any tendencies to be overly honest. While you certainly want to continue communicating in a truthful manner, there are times when the unadulterated truth can be hurtful. If, for example, you're asked whether you like your friend's new engagement ring, there is absolutely no point in telling her that you find it small and ordinary. You owe it to people to tell the truth when withholding it will cause negative consequences, but in many cases where the truth will not have any positive impact, it's permissible, and even desirable, not to be entirely honest. Giving an evasive answer or telling a white lie can be preferable under such circumstances.

Obviously, not all communication can be positive. Unpleasant or emotionally charged issues will sometimes have to be addressed. Even with the person you love most in the world, you won't always be happy and satisfied. You'll need to let him or her know how you feel so the situation has a chance of getting resolved. But it's a major (and extremely common) communication error to express this in a way that accuses, criticizes, blames or belittles the other person. Instead of addressing a complaint or concern in terms of what the listener has done wrong, you must learn to articulate simply how the behavior in question makes you feel. Change the focus from "you" to "I." For example, instead of saying, "You're spending too much money," you can rephrase it and say, "I get worried when we don't save some money every month." This changes the communication from a negative accusation to a neutral personal observation.

No matter how skilled you become at expressing yourself, it will all be in vain if you don't concern yourself with ensuring that the time and place is right for that communication. If the listener is tired or preoccupied, you need to be cognizant of this and adjust your communication accordingly. At these times, he or she may not appreciate a lot of idle chatter or a heavy discussion about something stressful. Intimate communication (ranging from declarations of love to an argument about money) will not be appropriate in certain places, such as at a dinner party with your boss, and should be reserved for more private circumstances.

It's up to you now to monitor your communication for errors you may be making. Look for the following:

- Communication without integrity.
- Overly honest communication.
- Negative communication.
- Communication at the wrong time or place.

The four worksheets that follow depict examples of each of these communication errors. After reading them, you can fill in the blank worksheet with an example of your own that occurred while communicating with a friend or partner. If you do this on a regular basis, you'll begin to recognize and avoid errors in communication. When you go for several months without any occurrences of communication errors, you can consider yourself to have reached an optimal level of communication skill. In terms of the very important area of communication, you'll be ready for love.

✳   ✳

COMMUNICATION ERROR: Communication without integrity.

DATE: October 20th

WHAT ACTUALLY HAPPENED: When a friend asked me if I could keep a secret, I said I could even though I knew I couldn't. What was told to me in the strictest confidence was then relayed to at least three other friends.

CONSEQUENCE: I felt terrible because I knew I had betrayed the friend who had confided in me. I'm now also very worried about it getting back to her. She'll know that I told other people and I could lose her friendship.

WHAT I SHOULD HAVE DONE DIFFERENTLY: Admitted that I have trouble keeping things to myself and discouraged her from confiding in me until I felt I could control my urge to gossip.

✳   ✳

�֍   ✱

COMMUNICATION ERROR: Overly honest communication.

DATE: September 3rd

WHAT ACTUALLY HAPPENED: My partner gave me a sweater for my birthday. I thought the colors were horrible. When he asked me how I liked it, I told him the truth.

CONSEQUENCE: He was hurt and angry, telling me that he doesn't feel he ever wants to buy anything for me again since I hate his taste.

WHAT I SHOULD HAVE DONE DIFFERENTLY: Told him that it's very different from what I normally wear, but that it's quite attractive. Tried it on and remarked that it's beautiful, but that I wasn't sure it was flattering on me. If he then said that I could return it if it wasn't quite right, I would be off the hook. If not, I could have kept it and worn it occasionally.

✱   ✱

✱   ✱

COMMUNICATION ERROR: Negative communication.

DATE: September 22nd

WHAT ACTUALLY HAPPENED: My partner came home late for dinner for the third time in a row. The second she walked in the door, I screamed, "Where have you been? Why didn't you call? Can't you ever think of anyone but yourself?"

CONSEQUENCE: She became angry and wouldn't speak to me for the rest of the night.

WHAT I SHOULD HAVE DONE DIFFERENTLY: Calmly told her that I worry when she's not home on time and that I'm disappointed when we can't have dinner together. Then I could have asked if we could work out a schedule where we would eat together three nights a week at a designated time that we both adhere to.

✱   ✱

✳ ✳

COMMUNICATION ERROR: Communication at the wrong time or place.

DATE: January 5th.

WHAT ACTUALLY HAPPENED: A friend ran into some hard times and has owed me money for several months. I met him and some of his co-workers for drinks after work. While we were drinking, I reminded him how long it's been since he borrowed that money.

CONSEQUENCE: My friend glared at me and said we would discuss it when we were alone. He paid me back a week later but told me that he didn't appreciate having his coworkers know that he was having financial trouble. Things haven't been the same between us since.

WHAT I SHOULD HAVE DONE DIFFERENTLY: Waited until I had the opportunity to speak to him privately.

✳ ✳

✳ ✳

COMMUNICATION ERROR: _____

DATE: _____

WHAT ACTUALLY HAPPENED: _____

_____

_____

_____

CONSEQUENCE: _____

_____

_____

WHAT I SHOULD HAVE DONE DIFFERENTLY: _____

_____

_____

_____

✳ ✳

Being able to communicate successfully won't automatically put love in your life or keep it there. But it *is* an absolutely essential aspect of your love ability. Once you become skilled in expressing what you think and feel to your partner and understand his or her thoughts and feelings, you'll be in a better position to find love and make the most of it.

RECOMMENDED READING

Beck, Aaron T. *Love Is Never Enough.* New York: Harper & Row, 1988.
Blaker, Karen. *Intimate Secrets: Which to Keep and Which to Tell.* Boston: Little, Brown, 1986.
Burns, David. *Intimate Connections.* New York: Morrow, 1985.
Tannen, Deborah. *That's Not What I Meant.* New York: Morrow, 1986.
———. *You Just Don't Understand.* New York: Morrow, 1990.

9

Can You Take a Lighthearted Approach to Love?

For love to work, it must be taken seriously. Love needs to be given the time, energy, and respect it deserves. Without a responsible and mature approach to love, both partners will be shortchanged.

But love should not be taken *too* seriously. It should not be treated like a business arrangement. Love should be fun. It needs to be savored as a joyous endeavor between two people. If love didn't lift the spirit, would there really be any point in pursuing it?

Obviously, a balanced approach is best. Love should be seen as both play and work. It calls for seriousness at times and playfulness at others. This chapter focuses on the ideal lighthearted approach to love. Take the quiz that follows to learn where you stand in terms of a lighthearted approach to life and love. Then read the strategies section to learn how to improve your abilities in this area.

✳ **Q U I Z** ✳

Answer each of the following questions honestly by selecting one response per question, without thinking about what they might reveal. You may be surprised at the results!

1. You and your partner are doing some grocery shopping. The store has been playing some nondescript background music, but then a new tape comes on. It's a catchy song that's always been one of your favorites. Your partner grabs you and begins dancing down the aisle. What do you do?
   a. Admonish him or her for being silly and break away. You might even escape to a different aisle and pretend you don't know him or her.
   b. Dance for a moment or two if you're alone in the aisle, but stop immediately if anyone else can see you.
   c. Enjoy dancing for the entire song and not worry about whether or not you're being watched.

2. How often do you take a "mental health day" from work and devote it to having fun rather than catching up on chores and running errands?
   a. Frequently (close to a day each month).
   b. Seldom (less than twice a year).
   c. Occasionally (about three to seven times a year).

3. What's your fantasy life like?
   a. You enjoy fantasizing from time to time, but keep your fantasies very private and wouldn't dream of acting them out.
   b. You rarely fantasize because you prefer to spend your time and energy on more practical pursuits.
   c. You have a very rich fantasy life and attempt to act out as many of them as you can.

4. Your typical thoughts on gift-giving are:
   a. Gifts should be practical. If the recipient doesn't really need it (or can't use it very often), it's just a waste of money.
   b. Save practical gifts for your grandmother and give everyone else *fun* gifts that they don't necessarily need but will love because it's something they wouldn't have bought for themselves.

c. Try to buy gifts that are both practical and fun at the same time.

5. Which type of movie or television show do you most like to watch?
   a. Comedy.
   b. Dramady (mixture of drama and comedy).
   c. Drama.

6. Your partner gets the giggles while the two of you are having sex. What's your reaction?
   a. Ask your partner what he or she finds so funny.
   b. Start laughing yourself and tease your partner by trying to make him or her laugh even more.
   c. Stop what you're doing and refuse to continue because you feel so indignant, annoyed and insulted.

7. How many hours of play or leisure time do you have on a typical weekday? Note that this does not include any work or household maintenance activities. It may include cooking or eating if done in a relaxed manner (rather than wolfing down fast food), shopping (if done strictly for fun), hobbies, games, sports, visiting with friends or not doing anything at all.
   a. More than five.
   b. One to five.
   c. Less than one.

8. Your partner gives you some very sexy underwear that is completely different from your usual style. How often would you wear it?
   a. Never. He or she should have known better.
   b. Occasionally. When you do, you'll make sure he or she sees it.
   c. Frequently. No one knows what you're wearing under your clothes, so you'll relish your little secret every time you wear it.

9. One of your friends is not very successful in the career world, but he thoroughly enjoys his life outside of work. In addition to having many friends and leisure interests, he manages to save enough from his extremely limited income to travel a few times a year. What do you feel toward this friend?
   a. Envy. He always seems to be having such a good time.
   b. Acceptance. His life-style and outlook wouldn't necessarily be right for you, but it is for him.

    c. Disdain. It's time he grew up and did something about establishing a real career.

10. A bomb threat has been called in to your place of work. Everyone has had to evacuate the building while it's checked out. It probably will take a couple of hours to investigate. What would you do in the meantime?
    a. Take a coffee break at a nearby restaurant, while checking regularly on the progress of the search.
    b. Go shopping for a few hours, figuring you won't be missed anytime soon.
    c. Catch up on some work while waiting outside.

11. If you had to baby-sit some kids, what would you be most likely to do with them?
    a. Watch them play.
    b. Play with them just as if you were a child yourself.
    c. Play with them while maintaining some distinct boundaries, with you as the adult.

12. How do you usually handle giving parties?
    a. You're stressed out at first, but finally relax about midway through when you see that the party is going well.
    b. You're too busy and worried to enjoy the party and collapse with relief when it's finally over.
    c. You love every moment of it from the planning to the actual partying and are never concerned that it won't go well.

13. If you were on your honeymoon (with someone you had just married or with your longtime spouse on a second honeymoon), you would:
    a. Wish it could go on forever.
    b. Be anxious for it to end so you could return to "real life."
    c. Enjoy every moment of it, but be ready to return home when it was over.

14. In your family, you were:
    a. The first-born or only child.
    b. The last-born ("the baby").
    c. The middle.

15. For each holiday, place a check under each category you've actually incorporated into your life this past year. For example, if you baked special heart-shaped cookies and wore red for Valentine's Day, you would check dress and food for that holiday. If you went to a fireworks demonstration on July Fourth or a party on Halloween, you would place a check in the events column for those holidays. Placed some shamrocks or green carnations on your table in March? If so, give yourself a check under the decor column for St. Patrick's Day. You may also have celebrated additional holidays and occasions this year, such as the first day of spring, Mardi Gras, Bastille Day or National Ice Cream Month. Write these down and check where appropriate.

	Dress	Food	Decor	Events
Valentine's Day				
St. Patrick's Day			WORE GREEN.	
Easter			PAINTED EGGS	
Fourth of July				
Halloween				
Thanksgiving				
Christmas/Chanukah/Kwanzaa				

16. Check every activity you've done in the past twelve months.

_____ Flew a kite

_____ Ordered a hot fudge sundae or ice cream soda

_____ Attended the circus

_____ Used a playground (e.g., swings or slides)

___✓___ Watched cartoons

___✓___ Took a bubblebath

_____ Baked cookies

_____ Collected shells on the beach

✓ Watched the sun rise

_____ Skated (ice or roller)

_____ Rode a merry-go-round

✓ Wore something silly that made people laugh or something startling that got their attention

✓ Stargazed, looking for specific stars or constellations

✓ Played with a pet that wasn't yours

_____ Created a handmade gift

_____ Went to the zoo

✓ Read a children's book

✓ Drank a cup of hot chocolate

✓ Played a board game

✓ Picked wildflowers

SCORING

Tally your points as follows:

1. a- 1   b- 3   c- 5
2. a- 5   b- 1   c- 3
3. a- 3   b- 1   c- 5
4. a- 1   b- 5   c- 3
5. a- 5   b- 3   c- 1
6. a- 3   b- 5   c- 1
7. a- 5   b- 3   c- 1
8. a- 1   b- 3   c- 5
9. a- 5   b- 3   c- 1
10. a- 3   b- 5   c- 1
11. a- 1   b- 5   c- 3
12. a- 3   b- 1   c- 5
13. a- 5   b- 1   c- 3
14. a- 1   b- 5   c- 3
15. and 16. Give yourself one point for each check.

Add up all your points, then turn to the profile indicated by your score.

  14 to   68—Serious
  69 to 109—Lighthearted
110 to 130—Frivolous

✳ Profiles

Read all about your approach to love and life in the profile that corresponds to your quiz score.

SERIOUS

You appear to take life quite seriously. There's probably a lot that you want to accomplish and you're determined to achieve all your goals. Chances are you're very self-motivated and don't need external reinforcement to pursue and realize your dreams and ambitions. You set out to do what must be done simply because you feel it's the right thing to do. Consequently, you rarely veer off the path you've chosen. Your approach to living your life is straightforward and disciplined.

This approach works well in most areas of the business world. It's highly likely that you have achieved considerable success in your work (or will in the near future, with continued hard work). But it's doubtful that you'll be as successful in the rest of your life. You won't live it to the fullest or enjoy it as much as people who can take things a little more lightly.

This is especially true in love. You're apt to become so bogged down with all the necessary but mundane details of your life that you forget about all the things that make love special. You lack the lighthearted approach to love and life that makes it all worthwhile. You may share a life with your partner, but you probably don't play much together. Instead of cultivating reasons and occasions to share a laugh or a playful moment, you tend to avoid them.

You may be excellent at shouldering responsibility and planning for the future, but you seem to neglect one of the more important duties in a romantic relationship: making it fun. Spontaneity, surprises and laughter may be missing in your relationship (unless your partner provides them and doesn't mind that you don't reciprocate). On the surface, it may look like the two of you have a wonderful life together, but you and your partner will sense from time to time that you don't quite have it all. You may have material success and a stable, committed relationship, but you're still missing an essential ingredient. Until you can let your guard down and let your inner child come out and play, you won't experience the sense of joy that the less serious know so well.

But it doesn't have to stay this way. Even as an adult, you can learn to play. You can become more ready for love by developing a lighthearted approach to love and life. Learn how in "Lightening Up on Love" in the strategies section.

LIGHTHEARTED

You've managed to find a happy medium between taking life and love too seriously and not taking it seriously enough. You know how to work at love, but you also know how and when to play at it. This balanced approach enables you to enjoy all that love can offer.

Where appropriate, you take things seriously. You recognize that everything can't always be fun and your maturity allows you to accept this. Hard work doesn't bother you. You're willing to do whatever it takes to be successful in love and life. You're probably able to plan ahead and organize yourself so you can accomplish both the short-term and long-term goals you and your partner have set for your lives. You wouldn't dream of doing anything frivolous that would endanger the stability of your relationship.

But this doesn't mean you're always methodical and solemn. You know when to let loose and deviate from what you've planned. You can take love lightly enough to allow for some flexibility and spontaneity. You're never too busy to laugh or play when the time is right. Your relationship will have plenty of mirth and merriment, which will keep love from ever becoming a drag.

Your lighthearted approach speaks well for your readiness for love. Although you don't need remedial education in this area, you still might benefit from reading the strategies section to develop your abilities further. If you scored at the low end of the lighthearted range, you'll want to pay particular attention to "Lightening Up on Love." If your score was on the high end of the range, you should concentrate on "Taking Love a Little More Seriously."

FRIVOLOUS

If there's one thing you know how to do, it's having fun. Wherever there's a good time to be had, you'll do everything within your power to take advantage of it. You probably have a large number of friends who relish that *joie de vivre*. They know they can always count on you to be cheerful and lively. Your upbeat nature ensures that everyone around you will enjoy themselves.

No matter what happens in your life, you're unlikely to lose your carefree ways. Nothing can get you down, at least not for very long. You know how to turn even the most negative circumstance around to salvage something good out of it. Your sense of humor can make anything seem a little less threatening or depressing.

But there is a point at which your playfulness becomes undesirable. Some things need to be taken seriously—love, for one. If you take it too lightly, you won't be able to do what it takes to nurture it. You'll play at love, but you won't work at it when you need to. Problems will go unresolved and true feelings will never be exposed. You and your partner may have a great time together, but mostly on a superficial level. Real intimacy will not develop unless you're willing to approach love in a serious manner when it's appropriate.

You're only kidding yourself if you think love can be fun all the time. You need to be willing to deal with the low points of love, instead of concentrating exclusively on the high spots. To fully share a life with someone, you need to deal with life as it really is, rather than trying to make it a nonstop party. No one would want you to lose your ebullience or your ability to have fun, but chances are your partner would appreciate not being the only one to assume responsibility and deal with some of the burdens and realities of everyday life.

You'll be more ready for love if you can learn to work at it instead of constantly playing at it. By "Taking Love a Little More Seriously" (as outlined in the strategies section), you'll acquire the ability to enjoy love in the most mature and responsible of ways.

✳ Strategies for Becoming More Lighthearted at Love

Read "Lightening Up on Love" if you tend to take love too seriously. If your approach to love can be frivolous, read "Taking Love a Little More Seriously."

LIGHTENING UP ON LOVE

Treating love too seriously will result in a businesslike partnership rather than an intimate romantic relationship. Focusing on the work needed to sustain love and ignoring the need for play may ensure that the two of you have a balanced checkbook or a beautifully decorated and sparklingly clean home, but it won't make life and love fun. While you can't (and shouldn't) cast your serious nature completely aside, you do need to learn to lighten up on love, even just a little, so both you and your partner enjoy it more.

Becoming more playful isn't easy to do. The natural ability you had as a child to find the magic in everyday life was lost as you became an adult. It will take some planning and determination to recapture some of that childlike joy, but you'll find the pleasure you gain is well worth the effort.

Play means different things to different people, so you'll have to determine what's right for you. Anything that brings even a momentary lifting of the spirit can qualify as lighthearted play. If it makes you and your partner laugh, exhilarates you, provides adventure and challenge, adds variety to your lives or celebrates life in both its ordinary and extraordinary aspects, it should be cultivated as a significant part of your life-style.

You're extremely well-organized and capable in incorporating work into your daily life. Unfortunately, you're much less skilled in scheduling time to play. Just as employers provide coffee breaks for their employees, you must provide a lighthearted break for yourself. No matter how busy you are with your job or household duties, this break should be a part of your day. To prevent "cheating" by forgetting to take your lighthearted break, you can even write it on your calendar or appointment book. Whether it's for twenty minutes on Tuesday around lunchtime or for an hour on Thursday evening, the break needs to be viewed as an important part of every day.

If you're absolutely convinced that you couldn't spare any time out of your busy schedule for play, you need to adjust your attitude and rearrange your priorities. You have twenty-four hours in each day, just like everyone else. How you choose to spend those hours is entirely up to you. By giving up something (whether it's extra time working, getting your nails done or cleaning your bathtub), you'll get something in return—freeing up time for play. You'll have to decide what's ultimately more important in your life: having fun with your partner, or work demands and a clean house.

Books and courses on time-management are readily available and can help you master your time better. You may find it worth the money to pay someone to take care of some of your responsibilities (e.g., housecleaning, balancing the checkbook or mowing the lawn) to give you extra time. Money, like time, is a finite resource you always feel you don't have enough of, but you can control how it's allocated. Instead of spending fifty dollars for a restaurant meal both you and your partner are too rushed and too tired to enjoy, it may be more pleasurable to have a twenty-dollar meal out if the rest of the money enables you to relax at home while someone else does the yard work.

The following exercise will help you plan a week's worth of lighthearted breaks. You'll commit yourself to a specific time as if you were setting up a dental appointment. You'll have to give up or rearrange what you would normally be doing at that time, and once you do that, you'll need to designate the type of play you'd like to do that day. Choose activities you and your partner will enjoy together but also save some time just for yourself where you do things that your partner wouldn't necessarily enjoy. After studying the example of the weekly break planner, fill out your own worksheet. Try to get in the habit of doing this every week.

✳   ✳

LIGHTHEARTED   BREAKS

SUNDAY
SCHEDULED FOR: 6 P.M. to 9 P.M.

TO BE GIVEN UP OR REARRANGED: Cooking dinner for in-laws.

TYPE OF PLAY: All of us grabbing a bite out and then going bowling.

MONDAY
SCHEDULED FOR: 5 P.M. to 6 P.M.

TO BE GIVEN UP OR REARRANGED: Catching up on mail at the office.

TYPE OF PLAY: Going out for happy hour.

TUESDAY
SCHEDULED FOR: 12 P.M. to 12:30 P.M.

TO BE GIVEN UP OR REARRANGED: Lunching with coworkers.

TYPE OF PLAY: Shopping for a "Just because I love you" gift for partner.

WEDNESDAY
SCHEDULED FOR: 8 P.M. to 9:30 P.M.

TO BE GIVEN UP OR REARRANGED: Club meeting.

TYPE OF PLAY: Relaxing in a hot tub, then reading a mystery novel.

THURSDAY
SCHEDULED FOR: 8 P.M. to 10 P.M.

TO BE GIVEN UP OR REARRANGED: Finishing report for work.

TYPE OF PLAY: Watching a video together.

FRIDAY
SCHEDULED FOR: 8:30 A.M. to 9:00 A.M.

TO BE GIVEN UP OR REARRANGED: Arriving at work before 8:30 A.M.

TYPE OF PLAY: Making love.

SATURDAY
SCHEDULED FOR: 9 A.M. to 1:30 P.M.

TO BE GIVEN UP: Cleaning the house.

TYPE OF PLAY: Taking a drive to the country with partner, having lunch out, and going antiquing.

✳   ✳

✳   ✳

L I G H T H E A R T E D   B R E A K S

SUNDAY
SCHEDULED FOR: _____

TO BE GIVEN UP OR REARRANGED: _____

_____

TYPE OF PLAY: _____

_____

MONDAY
SCHEDULED FOR: _____

TO BE GIVEN UP OR REARRANGED: _____

_____

TYPE OF PLAY: _____

_____

TUESDAY
SCHEDULED FOR: _____

TO BE GIVEN UP OR REARRANGED: _____

_____

TYPE OF PLAY: _____

_____

WEDNESDAY
  SCHEDULED FOR: _____

  TO BE GIVEN UP OR REARRANGED: _____

  _____

  TYPE OF PLAY: _____

  _____

THURSDAY
  SCHEDULED FOR: _____

  TO BE GIVEN UP OR REARRANGED: _____

  _____

  TYPE OF PLAY: _____

  _____

FRIDAY
  SCHEDULED FOR: _____

  TO BE GIVEN UP OR REARRANGED: _____

  _____

  TYPE OF PLAY: _____

  _____

SATURDAY
  SCHEDULED FOR: _____

  TO BE GIVEN UP OR REARRANGED: _____

  _____

  TYPE OF PLAY: _____

  _____

✳   ✳

Spontaneity is an important element of a lighthearted approach to love. Unexpected and unplanned activities can add excitement to your life together and renew your interest in each other. If you always follow a rigid schedule, you'll never have any spur-of-the-moment surprises that revive and renew romance. At first you may actually have to plan your spontaneity. This is somewhat of a contradiction in terms, but it may prove to be what you need initially until you become more comfortable with the real thing. You may need to set aside a time each week (such as Wednesday night or Saturday afternoon) to do whatever you feel like at that time.

Variety is another crucial aspect of playfulness. Be sure to incorporate this into your leisure time. Getting into a rut by always going out to the same restaurants or watching videos every Friday night is not conducive to an optimally lighthearted approach to love and life. Prevent yourself from becoming stagnant in your play by learning all you can about new places to go and things to do. Keep a notebook of possibilities that you can refer to when you get bored with the "same old thing."

Seek out opportunities to share a laugh with your partner. Enjoying humor together will add a glow to your dealings with each other. Laughter can bring you closer together and improve your outlook on life. Comedy clubs, movies, television, cartoons and books are good places to start.

But don't just rely on other people to bring you laughter. You can do it yourself by letting your inner child come out of hiding. By letting go of your inhibitions and participating in activities you may not have enjoyed since childhood, you'll rediscover fun in its purest form. Whether flying a kite or roller skating, don't be afraid to abandon your adult self. It's okay to be silly with the person you love.

Another way to play is to act out your fantasies. Encourage your partner to experiment with his or her dreams and desires, and do the same yourself. An atmosphere of acceptance will facilitate the process. If you both feel comfortable in your love, you shouldn't feel self-conscious about simulating your fantasies or actually trying to re-create them.

Celebration plays a big role in a lighthearted approach to love. By joyously acknowledging what's good or special in your lives, you mark those moments and forever etch them in your memory. When life gets boring or overly demanding, you can either call upon your recollections of happier times or find a reason to celebrate the positive that exists right now. Keep your eyes and ears open for events and occasions that other people celebrate. Libraries even have books that list holidays and celebrations around the world. Even the most exotic holidays celebrated halfway across the world can be fair game. You can also choose to acknowledge some humorous occasion such as National Pickle Week, or create your own traditions such as a "Wizard of Oz" party each year. Of course you won't want to neglect the big, traditional holidays. Instead of half-heartedly recognizing some holidays (such as giving the obligatory card for Valentine's Day), really do it up right by dressing for them, decorating, making appropriate foods and giving special gifts. Throw a party for two or twenty, depending on the mood you want to create.

If you're not currently in a love relationship, you can still adapt many of the suggestions offered in this section for solo use. It's important that you develop a lighthearted approach to life even when you're not romantically involved. When love develops, you'll be able to transfer your abilities to laugh and play from life to love. You'll also be more likely to attract people if you adopt a lighthearted, rather than an overly serious, perspective.

Take heart if learning how to play as an adult appears too difficult. It may not come naturally at first, but it will become second nature after a while. You'll never regret the effort you spent in learning to acquire a lighthearted approach to love.

TAKING LOVE A LITTLE MORE SERIOUSLY

A fun-loving approach to love and life is very desirable— you don't *ever* want to lose this ability. Without it, your relationship could become more of a duty than a joy. Love is meant to be pleasurable, and it's to your credit that you're so expert at enjoying it.

But, like anything else, it can be taken to an extreme. When this occurs, you're in danger of never taking anything seriously. Love can't be treated as a constant joke or a never-ending party. To do so is to neglect the nurturing quality of love. You're not being fair to either yourself or your partner if you view love as just fun and games.

You have the potential for going beyond healthy lightheartedness and entering the realm where you take a frivolous approach to love. To become more ready for love, you must learn to take it more seriously. By taking just a little more care with what you do and say, you can deal with love in a more mature, realistic and responsible way.

You need to address everything that impacts upon your relationship, including those things you'd rather not think about. Problems and responsibilities must be acknowledged rather than ignored. Instead of spending all your time and energy on the pursuit of fun, you can learn to divert some of it to working on love.

The following worksheet will require you to set aside time to work on love. After you pinpoint the specific problem or issue, you'll need to delineate some strategies for resolving the concern and then schedule time for each strategy. Read the examples and then fill out the blank worksheet on your own.

✳   ✳

PROBLEM OR ISSUE: Money troubles

STRATEGIES FOR RESOLUTION:
1. Discuss the solution with each other.
2. If we both agree, obtain credit counseling.

SCHEDULED FOR:
1. Discussion—Tuesday night
2. Credit counseling—next month

✳   ✳

✳   ✳

PROBLEM OR ISSUE: Interfering in-laws

STRATEGIES FOR RESOLUTION:
1. Discuss the situation with each other.
2. Read some self-help books on handling relatives.
3. Talk with the relatives about your feelings.

SCHEDULED FOR:
1. Discussion with each other—tomorrow at 10 A.M.
2. Reading—during the next three weeks
3. Family discussion—around the beginning of March

✳   ✳

❊   ❊

PROBLEM OR ISSUE: _____

STRATEGIES FOR RESOLUTION:

_____

_____

_____

SCHEDULED FOR:

_____

_____

_____

❊   ❊

Be sure to adhere to the scheduled time you allotted for the strategies on the worksheet. It will be very tempting to do something more fun than execute the strategies you've outlined at those designated times, but putting it off will mean the problem(s) will linger that much longer instead of being resolved. You also need to stick to anything else that you schedule with your partner. Once you commit yourself to something, you must follow through with it, even if something better comes along. It's permissible to be spontaneous once in a while, but your partner needs to feel you can be counted on too.

Jokes and pranks may be fun, but never at your partner's expense. You need to know exactly how much your partner can take and not exceed those limits. If your partner is to trust you, he or she must feel that you'll always consider his or her feelings and not do anything hurtful.

Even if you're not in a relationship right now, you should still concentrate on using these suggestions for the other areas of your life. Continue to enjoy yourself, but don't put off the hard work that needs to be done for you to solve your problems and reach your potential.

Love *should* be fun. You're already ahead of the game since

you know so well how to make love and life enjoyable. All you
have to do now is to take it a little more seriously.

RECOMMENDED READING

Belcher, William. *Intimate Play: Creating Romance in Everyday Life.*
    New York: Viking, 1987.

10

Can You Focus on Love in the Here-and-Now?

The past, present and future are all integral aspects of any person's life. Who you were yesterday affects who you are today and who you might be tomorrow. The past provides a foundation for the development of skills, attitudes and personality characteristics, while the future provides opportunity and direction for growth.

But it's the present that dominates our lives. The here-and-now is ultimately much more important than what happened in the past or what could happen in the future. This is especially true in love. A focus on the present enables a relationship to be enjoyed to its fullest, without dwelling on problems in the past or worries of the future. Living in the past or the future, if carried to an extreme, can interfere with your ability to love and be loved.

The quiz that follows will help you pinpoint which of the three time frames you emphasize in your life. You can then find the profile that describes how your time orientation affects your life and your love relationship. The final section details strategies for shifting the emphasis to the present.

---

*   # Q U I Z   *

For many of the following questions, you'll know which answers correspond to which time frame. But try to be honest in answering every question; there's absolutely nothing wrong with some of your responses falling in the past and future categories.

1. Of the following three choices, the music you like best is:
   a. Fifties to seventies rock.
   b. Current mainstream soft or hard rock.
   c. Space/New Age/New music.

2. If you had money to invest, your strategy for investing it in stocks or mutual funds would be based on:
   a. This year's performance.
   b. Their past performance over the last ten years.
   c. Projections for the future.

3. The car you would most like to have is:
   a. A futuristic sports car that runs on solar energy.
   b. An antique or "classic" automobile.
   c. A standard, middle-of-the-line model.

4. You tend to think most about:
   a. What you're involved in right now.
   b. What you will or might do in the future.
   c. What you've done or should have done in the past.

5. Your favorite vacation would be:
   a. Touring a historic city in the United States or Europe.
   b. Experiencing EPCOT Center at Disney World.
   c. Sunbathing at a Caribbean resort.

6. To try to keep healthy, you:
   a. Keep up with current medical knowledge and techniques.
   b. Follow the practices you learned from your parents and grandparents.
   c. Explore New Age health-promoting theories and practices, even if they're not proven to be effective or safe.

7. The television program you would prefer to watch is:
   a. A preview of a new show for next season.
   b. A current popular show.
   c. An old rerun of the *Honeymooners* or *I Love Lucy*.

8. To improve the environment, you would prefer that your tax dollars be used to:
   a. Restore something damaged or neglected.
   b. Start a new program that won't begin to show results for twenty years or more.
   c. Continue an environmental program to preserve the status quo.

9. The best part of a vacation is:
   a. Planning it.
   b. Actually experiencing it.
   c. Looking over the photographs after you've returned.

10. If you could live your life as if it were on a video recorder, your preferred mode would be:
    a. Rewind (and relive past experiences).
    b. Play (and live in the present).
    c. Fast-forward (and advance to the future).

11. Your preferred style of dressing is:
    a. Avant garde. You enjoy being ahead of the times.
    b. Classic. You like to wear the same styles you've worn for years.
    c. Current. You're most comfortable wearing what's popular.

12. The age group that you'd most like to perform volunteer work for is:
    a. The elderly.
    b. Adults.
    c. Children.

To find your total score, add up the points assigned to the answers you chose for the twelve questions.

1. a- 1	b- 3	c- 5
2. a- 3	b- 1	c- 5
3. a- 5	b- 1	c- 3
4. a- 6	b- 10	c- 2
5. a- 1	b- 5	c- 3
6. a- 3	b- 1	c- 5
7. a- 5	b- 3	c- 1
8. a- 1	b- 5	c- 3
9. a- 5	b- 3	c- 1
10. a- 3	b- 9	c- 15
11. a- 5	b- 1	c- 3
12. a- 1	b- 3	c- 5

(handwritten: 12, 20, 4, 9)

15 to 32—Past-oriented
33 to 56—Present-oriented
57 to 75—Future-oriented

✳ Profiles

Find the profile that reflects your time orientation

PAST-ORIENTED

You feel more comfortable with the past than you do with either the present or future. Most people have memories they savor from time to time, but you tend to review and relive prior experiences much more frequently. The uncertainty of the future may scare you, and the present may not match what you've enjoyed before, so you concentrate on the past.

But problems arise when you devote all your mental energies to the past, to the exclusion of the present and the future. You may try in vain to recapture the joys and successes of yesterday, eventually discovering it's impossible to recreate exactly what has happened before because the circumstances or people have changed. While you're chasing the past, you will have been ignoring the present and future. By not antic-ipating and planning for the future, you'll place yourself at a disadvantage and will find yourself unprepared when tomor-row becomes today. More importantly, you will have denied yourself the very real pleasures available in the present.

Living in the past can become extremely unhealthy when negative occurrences are rehashed over and over again. If you torment yourself with unpleasant memories you'll experience severe psychological pain that can totally interfere with your happiness in the present. However, the scope of this book does not permit discussion of pathological dwelling on the past; psychological self-help books and professional counseling are recommended for dealing with this problem.

When your past-orientation convinces you that the present or future can never be as good as what has already occurred, your ability to love and be loved will be compromised. If you're not currently in a love relationship, you may find yourself reluctant to become involved with anyone because he or she is not the same as (and therefore less appealing than) someone you may have been involved with before. Selective memory may persuade you that your past relationships were without any flaws or problems. If you believe things were perfect in the past, you'll have trouble accepting any imperfections in a current partner and relationship.

If you're past-oriented and in a relationship, you need to be careful not to let yesterday dominate today and tomorrow. A focus on the past will prevent you from growing as a couple because you won't take advantage of current opportunities that promote changes in your thoughts, feelings and actions. You won't expend sufficient energy into making today pleasur-able and meaningful. You'll also neglect making plans to achieve goals for the future.

To learn to shift your focus to the present, refer to the strategies section on "Leaving the Past Behind."

PRESENT-ORIENTED

You live in the present—and that's exactly where you should be. Enjoying the here-and-now enables you to get the most out of life and love. By concentrating on what happens as it happens, you focus your attention on each day as it unfolds. Instead of aimlessly dwelling on the past or anxiously anticipating the future, you're maximizing the most important aspect of time: the present.

Because you care about making *now* special and rewarding, you'll be sure to do everything possible to enhance a love relationship. When the right person comes along, you won't be bothered by ghosts from the past or dreams of the future; instead, you'll seize the moment and become involved without any reservations. Once you're in a relationship, you won't allow hurts or failures from the past to interfere with your love in the present. Nor will you become so entrenched with planning and worrying about tomorrow that you lose sight of living for today. You'll make the most of the relationship on a day-by-day basis.

As a present-oriented person, you're definitely ready for love. Just be careful not to neglect the past and future. Although not as important as the present, they both have implications for how you live your life today.

Occasionally take the time to review the past and its lessons. You can learn from mistakes you've made and avoid repeating them in the future. You also need to consider the future and plan for it. Totally living in the present without any thought about the years to come will prevent you from making and achieving long-term goals. Continue to emphasize the present but don't deny the importance of the past and future.

If you scored at the low end of the present-oriented scale, you should read "Leaving the Past Behind" in the strategies section. If you scored on the high end of this scale, turn to "Coming Back from the Future."

FUTURE-ORIENTED

The future intrigues you. Other people are threatened by the unknown, but you thrive on the possibilities of the yet-to-come. You already know the past and you're living the present, so it's the future that offers you the ultimate excitement and challenge.

There's a lot to be said for being future-oriented. Rather than occasionally wondering about the future like those who are present-oriented, you actually pursue it with enthusiasm and courage. You don't just wait for it to happen; you anticipate it and hasten its arrival. Whenever possible, you try to experience tomorrow today. Anything brand new or on the horizon appeals to you. You greatly admire the promise of what is to come and do whatever you can to accelerate its becoming a reality. You have dreams and visions for the future and work toward making them come true as quickly as they can.

The problem with a future orientation is you don't pay enough attention to what's happening today. You're likely to expend all your energy on planning for the future and never notice what's going on in the present. Thus you deprive yourself of the enjoyment of the here-and-now. You may currently be experiencing some success in love and life, but you won't appreciate it because you're concentrating on the future. It's very possible that some day you'll look back and wish you had made more of what was the present and has since become the past.

You may feel you're ready for love with your futuristic focus because you're prepared (or at least willing) to deal with whatever might happen. But love in the future is an abstract concept that doesn't provide tangible rewards. Only love in the present can offer real satisfaction. By neglecting the positive feelings and experiences as they occur, and by not taking advantage of opportunities to enhance your current enjoyment, you'll be losing out on the best parts of life and love.

As a future-oriented individual, you may have difficulty beginning a love relationship. You're apt to postpone getting involved with anyone because you're always waiting for someone better to come along. Eventually you might enter into a relationship, but at that point it may be more a reflection of your tiredness with being alone and putting your life on hold than of a real interest in your partner.

Fully loving and being loved by someone won't come easily to you. Instead of maximizing what you share in the present, you may be overly concerned about the future and work relentlessly to improve what might be instead of what actually is, right now. You may feel you're offering your partner security and happiness for the future, but what you're really doing is depriving him or her of love, present-tense. Worst of all, you may never notice or address current problems in the relationship because you're exclusively focusing on goals and plans for the future.

Read the strategies section on "Coming Back from the Future" to learn how to start living and loving today.

✳ Strategies for Living and Loving in the Present

By reading the appropriate section ("Leaving the Past Behind" if you're past-oriented and "Coming Back from the Future" if you're future-oriented), you can acquire the attitude and skills needed to make the most of love in the present.

LEAVING THE PAST BEHIND

Living in the past doesn't do much for life or love in the present. There are two basic ways your past-orientation can interfere with your getting the most out of today. These are:

- Becoming so nostalgic about the past, you convince yourself anything that happens now or in the future will never be as good as what you had yesterday.
- Focusing on the negative aspects of the past and not allowing yourself to move on to the present because you haven't resolved certain painful issues.

Read the section that pertains to your attitude about the past. If you yearn for what you had (or fantasize about what you had) in the past, "Stopping the Nostalgia Game" will show you how to put the past behind you. If you dwell on past problems, the tips in "Getting Beyond the Pain of the Past" are geared to you.

Stopping the Nostalgia Game

Nostalgia can be fun in small doses. Music, clothes and fads from the past can be remembered with fondness and bemusement. Memories from bygone days are capable of evoking a sense of comfort, especially if the past seems safer, less complicated or more pleasurable in some ways than life is today.

There's nothing wrong with nostalgia—unless it prevents you from enjoying the present. If you feel life was better then than it is now, you won't do much to help yourself in the present tense. Instead of concentrating on the most important part of life (the here-and-now), you'll be stuck in the past with memories that, though vivid, are still not the same as experiencing life as it actually happens. Trying to recapture the past will ultimately prove fruitless; you'll never succeed in recreating it because the people, times and things you hold so dear have not stood still. Change is inevitable, so it's not feasible to expect that anything will ever remain the same.

You don't have to give up memories of a past love that you cherish. But you do need to make sure that these memories don't take over your life. Excessive time spent in glorifying the past can prevent you from spending enough time appreciating the present. Love can become difficult when you're too focused on reliving old memories. You can't successfully find love if you reject people and experiences who are available in the present because they're not duplicates of what you once had. If you're in a relationship now, you won't be treating your partner fairly by holding on to the past with too tight a grasp. Focusing on the "good old days" and striving to recapture them won't allow your partner or your relationship to grow.

The worksheets that follow will enable you to pinpoint what you savor about the past and then determine what you need to give up from the past and what can be saved without interfering with the present. The most important step is the action plan, which commits you to doing something to enhance the present (thus effectively controlling your need for nostalgia about the past).

✳   ✳

I'M NOSTALGIC ABOUT THE PAST BECAUSE: When I was younger it was easy for me to get lots of dates.

IN CLINGING TO THE PAST, I SACRIFICE THE PRESENT: Not looking into why I'm now having trouble finding dating partners and not doing anything to help the situation.

I CAN KEEP FROM THE PAST WITHOUT SACRIFICING THE PRESENT: The confidence I used to feel when I met new people.

TO IMPROVE THE PRESENT, I NEED TO GIVE UP FROM THE PAST: My expectations that the right person will easily find me without my doing anything to make it happen.

MY ACTION PLAN FOR IMPROVING THE PRESENT: Putting more energy into finding love by joining activities and organizations where I might meet the type of person I want to date.

✳   ✳

This first worksheet provides the example of nostalgia about an easier time of dating when partners seemed to be more plentiful. A preoccupation with these nostalgic feelings will prevent introspective analysis about the reasons behind the current trouble finding dating partners and then taking steps to resolve the difficulty. The good thing about this aspect of the past and the memories it evokes is restoring the confidence once felt in meeting people. But all of the past cannot be retained. The expectation that the right partner will come along as if by magic needs to be discarded. In its place, the action step of joining activities and organizations to meet potential partners needs to be initiated.

---

*   *

I'M NOSTALGIC ABOUT THE PAST BECAUSE: I feel that we had a better relationship back when we first met.

IN CLINGING TO THE PAST, I SACRIFICE THE PRESENT BY: Not taking any action to improve my current relationship.

I CAN KEEP FROM THE PAST WITHOUT SACRIFICING THE PRESENT: Memories of the closeness we shared, which can inspire me to work toward improving the relationship (provided I don't try to make things exactly as they once were).

TO IMPROVE THE PRESENT, I NEED TO GIVE UP FROM THE PAST: Romanticizing about how things used to be; I need to recognize that things weren't perfect even when we were first together.

MY ACTION PLAN FOR IMPROVING THE PRESENT: Read self-help books on communication so I can facilitate more sharing of our thoughts and feelings.

*   *

On the second worksheet, nostalgia is focused on the perception that the relationship was better at its beginning. By dwelling on the past, no action is taken to improve the relationship as it is now. Memories of the closeness once shared can be retained only if there's no attempt at duplicating the past. The rewriting of the past in an overly romantic way needs to stop. The action plan for improving the present is to read self-help books on communication to enhance the sharing of thoughts and feelings.

As you write in your own responses on the blank worksheet, you'll need to give up those elements of the past that prevent your growth in the present and future. You can hold on to the parts of the past that don't sacrifice the present, but, difficult as it may seem at first, you will have to let go of some of the past, and substitute positive action for improving the present.

*

I'M NOSTALGIC ABOUT THE PAST BECAUSE: _____

_____

_____

IN CLINGING TO THE PAST, I SACRIFICE THE PRESENT BY:

_____

_____

_____

I CAN KEEP FROM THE PAST WITHOUT SACRIFICING THE PRESENT:

_____

_____

_____

TO IMPROVE THE PRESENT, I NEED TO GIVE UP FROM THE PAST:

_____

_____

_____

MY ACTION PLAN FOR IMPROVING THE PRESENT:

_____

_____

_____

*

Getting Beyond the Pain of the Past

Not everyone has a past that they found pleasurable. You may have endured some trauma or failure that continues to haunt you. Even though the memories hurt, it can be difficult to let go of some of the feelings from the past. Removing them from your active consciousness and reducing the past to a seldom-visited memory can require professional help, depending on the significance and pain associated with these events. If you've tried to rid yourself of the unpleasantness from the past and your failure to do so is robbing you of much pleasure in the present, you need to consider turning to a counselor for treatment.

If you've escaped any major trauma or deep-rooted psychological conflict but remain hung up on what went wrong, you can empower yourself to chip away at your preoccupation with the less desirable aspects of the past. The rewards of getting beyond it are obvious: The pain, self-doubts and negativity will be gone! You can start to feel good about yourself and life when you shift your focus to the present and stop torturing yourself with what was or should have been.

Functioning in the present mode will enable you to reap some pleasant benefits for your love life. Your ability to love and be loved will markedly improve when you concentrate your time and energy on making the present positive and rewarding.

The worksheets in this section will guide you in recording your feelings about the past and why it bothers you. You'll note how you sacrifice the present by clinging to the past. Then you're asked to differentiate the present from the past so you can see them as two totally separate entities that are not identical. Visualization is the next step; this enables you to rehearse mentally an improved present and future. The last step is recording a plan of action for turning what you've visualized into reality.

✳   ✳

WHAT BOTHERS ME ABOUT THE PAST IS: I would jump into a relationship too quickly and then get hurt later when it didn't work out.

IN CLINGING TO THE PAST, I SACRIFICE THE PRESENT BY: Being afraid now to take a chance on love since I've convinced myself that any relationship will end in failure.

I NEED TO RECOGNIZE THAT THE PRESENT IS DIFFERENT FROM THE PAST IN TERMS OF: My understanding that the mistakes I made can prevent me from repeating them.

WHEN I TRY TO VISUALIZE POSITIVELY WHAT THE PRESENT AND FUTURE CAN BE, I SEE: Myself slowly getting involved with someone whom I've gotten to know and trust.

TO MAKE THIS VISUALIZATION A REALITY, I WILL: Avoid the temptation of rushing into anything. Instead, I'll keep my options open and try to get to know people as friends first rather than as romantic partners.

✻   ✻

This first worksheet depicts a situation where the past has brought pain due to many failed relationships. The hurt experienced in the past may have inhibited any further attempts at finding love. But it helps to remember that the present is not the past and the mistakes previously made don't have to be repeated. (Human beings have a marvelous capacity to learn from their mistakes!) The visualization of slowly and successfully establishing intimacy can be put into action by refraining from continuing the past patterns of jumping into relationships too quickly.

✻   ✻

WHAT BOTHERS ME ABOUT THE PAST IS: That I was usually taken advantage of by my partner.

IN CLINGING TO THE PAST, I SACRIFICE THE PRESENT BY: Tormenting myself with what I should have done to make the situation better instead of actually taking any action to improve things.

I NEED TO REALIZE THAT THE PRESENT IS DIFFERENT FROM THE PAST IN TERMS OF: Both of us being older and (hopefully) wiser. My partner would probably be more willing to consider my needs now.

WHEN I TRY TO VISUALIZE POSITIVELY WHAT THE PRESENT AND FUTURE CAN BE, I SEE: A relationship filled with mutual consideration and respect.

TO MAKE THIS VISUALIZATION A REALITY, I WILL: Sit down with my partner once a week to discuss what we each want from our relationship and life together, and then find ways to meet both our needs.

✻   ✻

The second worksheet illustrates a preoccupation with negative feelings about being continually mistreated by a current partner. The constant focus on hurts of the past prevents any action from taking place in the present to improve the situation. Differentiating the past from the present reveals that a partner who was unwilling to change or compromise in the past may be willing to do so now. The visualization is of a relationship filled with mutual consideration and respect. To achieve what was visualized, a weekly discussion can be used to determine ways in which both partners can have their needs met.

Taking the time to fill out a blank worksheet to reflect your own situation is the first step for putting the past behind you. Don't deprive yourself of the opportunity to live and love in the present.

✳   ✳

WHAT BOTHERS ME ABOUT THE PAST IS: _____

_____

IN CLINGING TO THE PAST, I SACRIFICE THE PRESENT BY: _____

_____

I NEED TO REALIZE THAT THE PRESENT IS DIFFERENT FROM THE PAST IN TERMS OF: _____

_____

WHEN I TRY TO VISUALIZE POSITIVELY WHAT THE PRESENT AND FUTURE CAN BE, I SEE: _____

_____

TO MAKE THIS VISUALIZATION A REALITY, I WILL:

_____

_____

_____

✳   ✳

COMING BACK FROM THE FUTURE

An excessive emphasis on the future can limit your happiness in the present. There are three major ways in which your future focus can detract from the present:

- Putting your life on hold until a desired outcome (e.g., getting married or finishing school) is realized—preventing you from making the most of your life right now.
- Worrying about the future—interfering with your ability to enjoy the pleasures of the present.
- Focusing all your time and energy on long-term goals—depleting these resources for use in the here-and-now.

Although each area is addressed separately in this book, most future-oriented individuals demonstrate a combination of two or three problems. Read all three sections below so you can devise a plan that will work best for you.

Getting Your Life Off Hold

If you have a goal for the future that is extremely important to you, you may end up feeling life doesn't really begin until you arrive at the point you've set your sights on. Many singles, especially women, often believe this is true. Feeling their singlehood is just a transient state to be endured until they get married and their "real" lives begin, they delay fixing up their homes or perhaps buying a house. For some, marriage may be ten to twenty years away or may never happen at all, but they put off making decisions and taking action to improve their lives.

This procrastination can be found in various aspects of your life. Perhaps you'd like to get involved in a love relationship—but only after you lose fifteen pounds or get a promotion at work. You may be in a relationship currently but haven't done much about making any needed changes because you're waiting for something (e.g., to accumulate a down payment on a home, or the time when the kids move out) to occur first. Whatever your excuse is for not maximizing love and life in the present mode, you're denying yourself and your partner much of the satisfaction that today can bring.

Setting goals comes easily for you. What's far more difficult is making the most of the process of achieving them. Without losing sight of what you want to achieve in the future, you need to concentrate on living for today. Take time to consider what you may be losing by putting everything on hold until you reach your goals.

The following worksheets will help you sort out your goals, what you've been sacrificing along the way for that goal attainment, and how you plan to add what's missing in the present tense to your life or your relationship.

✳   ✳

MY GOAL IS: To have a long-lasting, committed relationship with someone.

I'LL KNOW I'VE REACHED MY GOAL WHEN: We see each other exclusively for a year or more.

WHILE TRYING TO REACH MY GOAL, I'VE SACRIFICED: Getting to know many interesting people because I've immediately ruled out those who I felt wouldn't be able to commit themselves to the type of relationship I'm looking for.

I WANT TO INCLUDE THE FOLLOWING IN MY LIFE, EVEN BEFORE I REACH MY GOAL: A greater number and enhanced variety of people in my social network, thus increasing my chances of eventually finding the right person and of enjoying some good company in the meantime.

MY ACTION PLAN TO START INCORPORATING THIS IN MY LIFE IS: Attend recreational and civic organization meetings so I can meet a variety of people. I'll get to know a few of them better before I decide they're not worth my while.

✳   ✳

This first worksheet illustrates the example of someone who wants a permanent, serious relationship and has been unwilling to get to know anyone who doesn't seem interested in this type of relationship. The change that needs to be made is to expand the social network to increase the opportunities for meeting that special someone, as well as to establish more friendships to be enjoyed in the present. Attendance at club meetings could be used to accomplish this, in addition to developing a more open mind about new people.

✻   ✻

MY GOAL IS: To try to save up enough money to open up my own business.

I'LL KNOW I'VE REACHED MY GOAL WHEN: I have $30,000 saved.

WHILE TRYING TO REACH MY GOAL, I'VE SACRIFICED: Spending money on gifts, entertainment, vacations, and other purchases that my partner and I could enjoy together.

I WANT TO INCLUDE THE FOLLOWING IN MY LIFE, EVEN BEFORE I REACH MY GOAL: One romantic day or night with my partner every week.

MY ACTION PLAN TO START INCORPORATING THIS IN MY LIFE IS: Setting aside $75 each week for restaurants, night clubs, trips to the country, etc.

✻   ✻

The second worksheet depicts a long-term goal of accumulating enough capital to start up a business. The problem is your enjoyment of the present has been severely curtailed since every cent has been going toward this goal. To make the most of a relationship in the here-and-now, even before the goal is reached, the action plan specifies setting aside seventy-five dollars each week for some romantic times together.

In the first example, love has been difficult to find because of the extreme focus on a future goal; in the second example, love and romance have not been fully enjoyed since all money has been diverted to reach a goal in the distant future. Use the blank worksheet to pinpoint what you've been sacrificing while striving for your future goal and commit yourself to making some changes to make love and life better *now*.

```
* ─────────────────────────────────────────── *

  MY GOAL IS: _____

  _____

  I'LL KNOW I'VE REACHED MY GOAL WHEN: _____

  _____

  WHILE TRYING TO REACH MY GOAL, I'VE SACRIFICED:

  _____

  _____

  I WANT TO INCLUDE THE FOLLOWING IN MY LIFE, EVEN BEFORE I
  REACH MY GOAL: _____

  _____

  MY ACTION PLAN TO START INCORPORATING THIS IN MY LIFE IS:
  _____

  _____

  _____

* ─────────────────────────────────────────── *
```

Ending Your Worries About the Future

Are you so worried about the future that you can't enjoy the present? This is an unfortunate problem for many people. They dwell on possible calamities that may happen in the future. Sometimes this is done deliberately in an attempt to prepare for the worst. They feel it's important to mentally rehearse future events so they'll be better equipped to deal with them if and when they occur.

This way of thinking appears to have some credibility, but it usually turns out to be unsuccessful. All the preparation for possible disaster may fall by the wayside when that disaster becomes a reality. Emotionally, you'll feel just as much distress as if you had never rehearsed it in your mind. The turmoil at the time could wipe out the plans you made beforehand and you still may be confused about what to do next.

In the meantime, you'll succeed only in torturing yourself about what may never even happen. Your worries will rob you of the enjoyment that may be available to you in the present. Today's wonderful opportunities and pleasures may be overlooked as you concentrate on tomorrow's potential difficulties.

You definitely want to prevent your anxieties about the future from spoiling a relationship you have today. Making love special has to happen in the here-and-now; it can't be put off indefinitely. By the time you finally get around to doing something to improve things, it may be too late to revive a relationship that's withered from neglect.

The worksheets that follow will help you resolve your preoccupation with the "what-ifs." After acknowledging your worries, you can then ask yourself "So what if it does happen?" Once you determine the worst thing that can happen, you may realize it wouldn't be quite as disastrous as you had originally anticipated. You can then figure out how to improve the situation if it should occur. After these three steps, you can make a resolution to focus your energy on what's currently happening in your life.

The first worksheet offers the example of someone who is not yet in a relationship and has some fears about getting involved. The second worksheet touches on the worries someone in an ongoing relationship may have. After reviewing these two pages, use the blank worksheet to record your worries about the future and to plan for a better today.

✳   ✳

MY WORRIES ABOUT THE FUTURE ARE: I'll become involved with someone who isn't right for me.

IF THIS HAPPENS, THE WORST CONSEQUENCE WOULD BE: I would have "wasted" a few months in a relationship that didn't work out and would have to start all over again with someone else.

TO MAKE THINGS BETTER IF IT DOES HAPPEN, I COULD: End the relationship immediately and begin to meet other people.

UNTIL THEN, I'LL FOCUS MY ENERGY ON: Enjoying meeting and getting to know people. If a relationship develops, I'll let it happen without worrying about it and reevaluate the situation if it doesn't feel right.

✳   ✳

✳   ✳

MY WORRIES ABOUT THE FUTURE ARE: My partner and I may grow apart.

IF THIS HAPPENS, THE WORST CONSEQUENCE WOULD BE: A mutual agreement to end the relationship.

TO MAKE THINGS BETTER IF IT SHOULD HAPPEN, I COULD: Obtain professional counseling to see if there's any way to save the relationship. If we do split up, I'll continue to pursue my life and possibly enter into another relationship.

UNTIL THEN, I'LL FOCUS MY ENERGY ON: Finding more ways to share our lives and interests with each other.

✳   ✳

✳   ✳

MY WORRIES ABOUT THE FUTURE ARE: _____

_____

IF THIS HAPPENS, THE WORST CONSEQUENCE WOULD BE:

_____

TO MAKE THINGS BETTER IF IT SHOULD HAPPEN, I COULD:

_____

UNTIL THEN, I'LL FOCUS MY ENERGY ON: _____

_____

_____

✳   ✳

Focusing Some Time and Energy on the Present

As a future-oriented person, you probably devote most of your time and energy to the possibilities presented by the future. The problem is that each of us have a finite amount of these two commodities. There's only so much allotted to each individual. If we use all our time and energy in one area, we won't have any left for anything else.

Focusing on the future can leave you with little or no time and energy for the present. While you may find it fulfilling to think, plan and work toward long-term goals, you're still cheating yourself out of experiencing what's happening right now. If you end up not achieving your goals in the future, you may find yourself wishing you had given a little less to the future and more to what had been the present. Even if you do reach the goals you had set for yourself, you may find their attainment to be less satisfying than you had envisioned. Looking back, you may begin to realize those long-term goals weren't really all that important.

Your relationship can wither if you don't put sufficient time and energy into making it special. If you're not in a relationship but are trying to find love, your chances of finding it are diminished by the lack of time and energy you've committed to this quest. Love can blossom and grow only with those two essential ingredients.

The next worksheet requires you to record where you're devoting your time and energy in terms of future goals or possibilities. Once you realize where and how they're overutilized, you can pinpoint where they're lacking in the present. To complete the exercise, you'll need to devise an action plan for allotting your time and energy in a more balanced fashion.

The first worksheet illustrates someone who is searching for love but feels love can only be found when physical perfection is achieved, thus necessitating the expenditure of excessive time and energy in working out. The preoccupation with exercise robs the present of time and energy for participation in other activities, which in turn limits opportunities for meeting a potential partner. The plan for improving the imbalance is to curtail workouts to a few times each week and use the saved time and energy for enjoying other activities.

Finding love is not the issue in the second worksheet. Instead, the problem is that excessive time and energy focused on work (and achieving a promotion or other career advancement in the future) creates a drain on time for enjoying life in the present with a partner. There is no magic solution to this imbalance; the only solution is to shift some time and energy away from work and into some quality time with the partner.

✳   ✳

THE GOAL(S) OR ASPECT(S) OF THE FUTURE THAT I DEVOTE MUCH OF MY TIME AND ENERGY TO IS: Physical fitness, which causes me to devote myself to working out so people will find me attractive (read "lovable").

THIS DEPLETES MY TIME AND ENERGY IN THE PRESENT FOR: Participating in any other activities besides exercise, thereby denying me opportunities to meet and connect with someone special.

TO REMEDY THIS IMBALANCE, I CAN: Resolve to work out only three nights a week and use the rest of my time and energy for enjoying other activities and increasing my social network. I also need to remind myself that I don't need a 100% perfect body to find and keep love.

✳   ✳

✳   ✳

THE GOAL(S) OR ASPECT(S) OF THE FUTURE THAT I DEVOTE MUCH OF MY TIME AND ENERGY TO IS: Working sixty-plus hours a week to advance my career.

THIS DEPLETES MY TIME AND ENERGY IN THE PRESENT FOR: Sharing a life with my partner.

TO REMEDY THIS IMBALANCE, I CAN: Cut back my time at the office to forty-five hours a week, work another five hours at home, and reserve at least ten hours weekly to spend with my partner.

✳   ✳

```
✳                                                                    ✳
  THE GOAL(S) AND ASPECT(S) OF THE FUTURE THAT I DEVOTE
  MUCH OF MY TIME AND ENERGY TO IS:

  _____

  _____


  THIS DEPLETES MY TIME AND ENERGY IN THE PRESENT FOR:

  _____

  _____


  TO REMEDY THIS IMBALANCE, I CAN: _____

  _____

  _____

  _____
✳                                                                    ✳
```

By determining how you're robbing your present of the time and energy needed to make it rewarding, you begin to refocus your priorities. You may not be able to change the past or control what happens in the future, but you can improve living and loving today by emphasizing the present.

RECOMMENDED READING

Adams, Jane. *Wake Up, Sleeping Beauty: How to Start Living Happily Ever After—Right Now.* New York: Morrow, 1990.

Freeman, Arthur, and Rose De Wolf. *Woulda/Coulda/Shoulda.* New York: Morrow, 1989.

Are You Ready for Love?

Each of the preceding ten chapters examined an aspect of love ability in isolation. Once you've taken all the quizzes, you can obtain an estimate of your overall readiness for love. Review your score in each chapter to pinpoint those areas where you scored in the middle range. Check all the descriptions that apply to you, as indicated by the score you received in each respective chapter.

☐ risk-evaluator   (Chapter 1)

☐ realistic   (Chapter 2)

☐ committed   (Chapter 3)

☐ adequate room (for love)   (Chapter 4)

☐ user (of money)   (Chapter 5)

☐ giver-receiver (of sexual pleasure)   (Chapter 6)

☐ self-oriented and other-oriented   (Chapter 7)

☐ communicative   (Chapter 8)

☐ lighthearted   (Chapter 9)

☐ present-oriented   (Chapter 10)

How many were you able to check off?

9 to 10

Congratulations! You should be very successful in finding and keeping love. But do resist the temptation to become too complacent. Scoring so well today doesn't necessarily mean you'll be at exactly the same level in the future. People do change, so you'll need to monitor your abilities and characteristics and make improvements as needed.

7 to 8

You're ready for love. You haven't yet mastered all of the components, but you're well on your way. You're already in a better position to enjoy love than are most people. By devoting some additional time and energy to further developing your love ability, you'll reach an enviable level of readiness.

5 to 6

You're not entirely ready for love, but you're at least half-way there. A romantic relationship will probably not proceed smoothly at times since you have not fully developed your love ability. But you do have the potential to love and be loved, especially if you devote yourself to enhancing those characteristics profiled in the chapter in which you did not score in the middle range.

3 to 4

You'll need to make some changes before you can expect love to work for you. If you're not receptive to making those changes, then you'll need to question whether you really want love in your life. You have a long way to go until you can make the most of a relationship. But if you really want to love and be loved, you'll see your score as a challenge rather than an obstacle. The personal and romantic growth you'll realize when you improve your readiness for love will be well worth the effort.

1 to 2

Just because your score is low doesn't mean love is out of the picture for you. You're as entitled to be loved and to love as anyone else. But your score should alert you to the likelihood of encountering many problems in love . . . until you develop more readiness for it. If you're not currently in a relationship, you may want to delay becoming romantically involved until you make some changes. If you are in a relationship, you'll need to apply yourself diligently to increasing your readiness for love. Don't get discouraged; just realize that love won't come easily to you for a while. Work hard at gaining the traits that will empower you to find and keep love in your life.

You shouldn't be alarmed if you ended up with less than ten checks. To be successful in love, you don't have to score a "perfect 10." What's important is that you had enough interest and motivation to use this book to assess your love ability. Regardless of your current score, there is always the potential to improve your functioning. The strategies sections in this book and the recommended readings can help you become more ready for love. Take the quizzes six months from now and see how you've changed. Your love life is much too important to neglect!